THE ESSENCE OF SPIRITUALITY

S. RAMKUMAR

ISBN 979-8-89632-337-2

DEDICATION

This book is dedicated with heartfelt appreciation to Anoop Jaiswal, former DGP of Tamil Nadu, whose kindness and altruistic nature have been a guiding light on my journey, and in memory of Late Mrs Radha Burnier, a distinguished Theosophist and former President of the Theosophical Society, Adyar, whose profound knowledge, compassion, and wisdom have been an enduring source of inspiration.

Contents

SHANTI MANTRA – MANTRA OF PEACE

Om asato ma sadgamaya

Tamaso ma jyotirgamaya

mrtyorma amrtam gamaya

Om shanti shanti shanti.

ॐ असतो मा सद्गमय ।
तमसो मा ज्योतिर्गमय ।
मृत्योर्मा अमृतं गमय ।
ॐ शान्तिः शान्तिः शान्तिः ॥

Lead me from the asat to the sat.

Lead me from darkness to light.

Lead me from death to immortality.

Om Peace Peace Peace.

(Brihadaranyaka Upanishad — I.iii.28)

Foreword

In an era of unprecedented material advancements and relentless pace, there is an ever-deepening hunger for meaning, connection, and inner peace. *The Essence of Spirituality* by Mr. S. Ramkumar emerges as a luminous guide for those navigating the complexities of modern existence while yearning for a deeper connection with the Self and the Universe. He is the author of two other popular books: *Not Just A Joke Book* and *Wit, Wisdom and Everything In Between*.

This book is more than a collection of thoughts on spirituality; it is a heartfelt journey that intertwines personal experiences, universal truths, and timeless wisdom. Drawing upon the teachings of revered spiritual luminaries, such as, J. Krishnamurti, Swami Chinmayananda, Mahatria Ra, Radha Burnier, and others, the author presents a path that bridges ancient traditions and contemporary understanding. From the foundational principles of Sanatana Dharma to the transformative power of gratitude, meditation, and faith, the chapters unfold as gentle invitations to explore the profound potential of the spirit within.

The author's journey itself — transitioning from a successful career in business to a life immersed in spiritual inquiry and selfless service — resonates deeply with the challenges faced by those seeking purpose beyond achievement. It reminds one that true fulfilment is not found in outward accomplishments but in embracing our inner light, living in harmony with universal principles, and cultivating love, compassion, and equanimity in our daily lives.

What sets *The Essence of Spirituality* apart is its accessibility. Complex concepts are rendered into relatable insights, enriched by inspiring anecdotes and practical applications. Whether one is new to spiritual exploration or a seasoned seeker, this work offers a treasure trove of wisdom to inspire and guide.

It is hoped that this book will serve as a companion for the reader's spiritual journey, igniting the spark of self-awareness and guiding him/ her toward a life of balance, peace, and universal connection. As one turns its pages, may one find clarity, strength, and the courage to embrace his true Self.

Mr. Ramkumar is a dear friend and a fellow member of The Theosophical Society. I wish him and his book all success.

Dr. Chittaranjan Satapathy, IRS(Retd.)
Former International Vice-President of The
Theosophical Society.

Inspiration and Acknowledgement

I extend my heartfelt gratitude to the luminaries and institutions whose profound talks, writings, and exemplary lives have deeply enriched my understanding of life and spirituality, leaving an indelible mark on my spiritual journey.

1. **Swami Gauthamananda** (President, Sri Ramakrishna Mutt) – A revered spiritual leader who has served the Ramakrishna Mutt in various capacities. Renowned for his social work and kindness, he embodies the principles of service to humanity, devotion (Bhakti), gratitude, non-attachment, humility, purity, courage, and faith. His teachings, along with the Mutt's philosophy of "God is one, but paths are many," have instilled in me a profound respect for all religions and a deep belief in universal harmony.

2. **Radha Burnier** – Former President of The Theosophical Society, she exemplified the ideals of oneness, compassion, empathy, simplicity, and spirituality. Her unwavering commitment

to living the values she taught has inspired me to integrate these principles into my daily life.

3. **Swami Chinmayananda** – The esteemed spiritual leader and founder of Chinmaya Mission, whose timeless teachings have enhanced my understanding of self-awareness, inner transformation, emotional intelligence, and equanimity. His BMI (Body-Mind-Intellect) framework has illuminated the interconnectedness of life, while his emphasis on prioritization and service continues to guide me.

4. **J. Krishnamurti** – A visionary philosopher and spiritual thinker, whose profound teachings on freedom from conditioning, total responsibility, and self-awareness have shaped my ability to observe thoughts, emotions, and actions without judgment. His insights have fostered a deeper connection with my true self and a heightened sense of inner clarity.

5. **Mahatria Ra** – A spiritual teacher, philosopher, and founder of Infinitheism, a movement dedicated to holistic growth. His profound insights into God, meditation, living in the present, spiritual evolution, raising energy levels, faith, and life leadership have been a beacon of light on my journey of self-discovery and purposeful living.

6. **Anoop Jaiswal, IPS** – Former DGP of Tamil Nadu, whose altruistic nature, kindness, humility, and ability to view situations from others' perspectives have been truly inspiring. His straightforwardness, courage, simple living coupled with high thinking, consistent good behavior, and love for learning have left a lasting impression on me.

7. **Dr. Chittaranjan Satapathy,** – Former International Secretary of The Theosophical Society and former Commissioner of Customs, Bombay Airport. His diligence, courage, service to humanity, uprightness, humility, and deep knowledge of Theosophy—synthesizing spirituality, religion, and science—have greatly influenced me. His ability to apply these principles to everyday life, combined with his simplicity and insatiable curiosity, continues to inspire.

Disclaimer

The content of *The Essence of Spirituality*, is intended to provide insights, reflections, and guidance on spiritual growth and well-being. It is based on the author's personal experiences, interpretations, and understanding of spirituality.

This book is not intended to replace professional advice, therapy, or religious teachings. Readers are encouraged to explore and adapt the concepts presented here according to their own beliefs, practices, and discernment.

The author and publisher are not responsible for any actions taken based on the ideas shared in this book. Spirituality is a deeply personal journey, and individual experiences may vary.

Preface

I have an experience of around 25 years in the turnkey interiors business, working with corporate clients and showrooms. In 2010, when I was 52, I decided to close that chapter because I was not getting fulfilment in the material realm at that point. Once goals are achieved, they lose their power to motivate; feeling satisfied and content at that stage of life left me without further drive in that area. That was when I joined the Theosophical Society and Ramakrishna Mutt to serve and contribute in ways that drew on my education, experience, and skills.

A friend, after catching up with me about my new role, shared in our alumni network, "Ramkumar has become a spiritual person!" This made me reflect on what that really meant. Through conversations with monks and theosophists, I came to understand that spirituality starts with purity—purity of thoughts and feelings. Service, love, and other values lie at the heart of spirituality, as this book will explore in depth.

This book aims to convey that self-actualisation involves engaging meaningfully with the outer world while staying connected to the spirit within.

King Janaka exemplified this balance—living as both a king and a sage, he pursued wealth without attachment to it. We too can aspire to lead life in the spirit of King Janaka, harmonising worldly aspirations with inner detachment.

Living life in this world is much like flying a kite. The kite flier, grounded on earth, aims to lift the kite high. But for the kite to soar as intended, he must stay grounded rather than running around, trusting in his skills and patience to guide it along the desired path.

In a world often defined by the relentless pursuit of the material, this book, *Spirituality*, invites readers to explore the boundless realm of the spirit—a journey beyond mere existence. The heart of this work resonates with a call to recognise the divine essence that permeates every life and to find purpose that transcends the ephemeral pleasures and pains of our daily lives.

Spirituality doesn't mean abandoning work to pray or escaping to the mountains to meditate. Instead, it's about understanding that life begins with spirit. Every living being, anything with life, is rooted in spirit, and that is formless. Since we can't see or define the formless directly, we create forms to relate to it.

Work brings meaning to life, and approaching it with a Karma Yoga mindset—focusing on serving a greater good—enhances that meaning. When we do our work with intention and a positive attitude, aiming to benefit our community and the world, we inevitably benefit ourselves as well.

Across the chapters, profound ideas unfold on themes such as the nature of God, the essence of Dharma, the pursuit of purpose, and the power of beliefs. Each chapter gently guides the reader deeper into questions that have occupied humankind for millennia: Who is God? Why are we here? How do we align our lives with a universal purpose? And, perhaps most significantly, how do we cultivate a spirituality that is not bound by dogma but is expansive, inclusive, and profoundly human?

The spiritual energy or eternal spirit, as explored through Sanatana Dharma and other philosophical traditions, is the essence of life itself, the unseen thread that binds all existence. Moving through the chapters, we see how spirituality is not a doctrine but a way of being, a personal journey of alignment with the divine principles that underpin existence. Through stories, analogies, and reflections, the narrative illuminates spirituality as the "current" that guides our lives, moving us towards inner peace, purpose, and connection with all beings.

The journey through this book is not about answers alone. It is about awakening to a larger perspective, a way of viewing oneself not as an isolated individual but as an integral part of a universal whole. The exploration of beliefs, their power, and their transformative potential reminds us that reality is often shaped by what we hold to be true, urging readers to believe in their highest potential and act accordingly.

In presenting spirituality as an inclusive path, this book recognises that each individual's journey is unique, shaped by experiences, aspirations, and inner callings. This is spirituality not as an abstract ideal but as a living, breathing force—one that, when consciously embraced, transforms not only individual lives but also the world we share.

May this book, *The Essence of Spirituality* serve as a companion on your path to discovering the true nature of self, spirit, and universe. May it inspire a deeper alignment with the eternal truths that unite us all and bring forth the peace, love, and fulfilment that lies within.

Introduction
Embracing the Soulful Journey

In a world that is constantly shifting, where the pressures of daily life often obscure our inner voice, the quest for happiness, peace, clarity, and purpose has never been more essential. This book, "The Essence of Spirituality" Journey, seeks to serve as a guide through the landscapes of spirituality, drawing on timeless wisdom and practical insights to illuminate the path toward deeper understanding and fulfilment. From the essence of body, mind, and intellect to the profound realms of self-realisation, each chapter is a stepping stone on a pathway that brings us closer to our true self.

Our journey begins with the foundations of holistic well-being, inviting us to explore the interconnectedness of our physical, mental, and spiritual dimensions. From these roots, we embark on a transformative voyage – one that gently nudges us to shift perspectives, uncover the joy within, and establish a stable foundation of faith and tranquillity.

The middle stages of our journey encourage self-realisation, asking us to transcend the ego, to discern between fleeting desires and lasting wisdom, and to embrace both the solitude and oneness that are inherent to our spiritual nature. Drawing on the principles of Sanatana Dharma and cultivating a deeper awareness of life's timeless truths, we open ourselves to a profound transformation.

In the later chapters, we turn towards growth practices – gratitude, meditation, and union with the self. Here, we explore the nature of the spirit, delve into the significance of ancient practices like the Gayatri Mantra and Yoga, and contemplate the concept of divinity itself. Each practice is a key, unlocking new levels of insight and understanding.

Finally, as we approach the summit of advanced spirituality, we reflect on the beauty of uncertainty, the guiding light of our conscience, and the purpose of life. As we grow, we integrate spiritual principles into our everyday reality, awakening a state of oneness and evolving toward our highest potential.

'"The Essence of Spirituality" is an invitation to explore, reflect, and embrace each stage of spiritual growth, transforming the journey itself into a source of strength, wisdom, and peace. Through self-discovery, we find not only our purpose but also a renewed, enduring connection to the divine essence which is within all of us.'

Key takeaways from the Essence of Spirituality include:

Foundation (Chapters 1-5)

These chapters set the stage for understanding and cultivating inner peace and well-being by connecting the physical, mental, and spiritual realms.

1. B, M, I: The BMI chart explains the whole theme of our lives represented by body, mind, intellect as the equipment. O, E, T are the objects of experience represented by objects, emotions, and thoughts. P, F, T are the representation of ego and are represented by perceiver, feeler, and thinker. V is the Vasanas, and OM is Absolute Reality or God.

   - The BMI chart of Swami Chinmayananda offers valuable insights into the human experience, helping us understand ourselves better. It's based on the principles of Vedanta and provides a simple visualisation of how our thoughts, actions, and happiness are influenced by various factors. Discover the interconnectedness of body, mind, and intellect.

   - The chart also highlights the role of Vasanas, our innate urges and past tendencies, which influence our experiences[3] [4]. By understanding and transcending these Vasanas, we can realise our true Self, represented by OM, the Supreme Reality.

Overall, the BMI chart offers a profound framework for self-reflection, personal growth, and spiritual evolution.

2. The Journey to Self-Discovery: Setting Intentions

    - Explore the power of clear intentions for self-discovery.

    - Gain clarity on values and purpose.

3. Happiness is Inside, Not Outside: Shift in Perspective.

    - Redefine happiness as a state within, independent of external achievements.

    - Embrace contentment as an inner choice.

4. Faith: Is the knowledge of the heart beyond the reach of proof.

    - Cultivate trust in life's journey and unseen forces.

    - Understand faith as a stabilising force in times of doubt.

5. Finding Tranquillity Amidst Chaos: Establishing Inner Peace

    - Learn techniques to stay calm in turbulent environments.

    - Experience peace as an inner sanctuary amidst life's changes.

Self-Realisation (Chapters 6-12)

This section moves into deeper aspects of the self, encouraging transcendence and inner growth.

1. Transcending Ego: The art of "letting go."

   - Recognise and release the grip of ego on self-identity.

   - Practice humility and self-awareness as pathways to authenticity.

2. Internal vs. External Power: Sakthi vs. Durga – Empowerment.

   - Distinguish between external accomplishments and inner power.

   - Cultivate true empowerment from within.

3. Discrimination, Desire-lessness, Love, Wisdom: The Four Pillars of Growth

   - Develop discernment, simplicity, compassion, and insight.

   - Use these qualities as guides on your spiritual path.

4. Daily Loss and Moving Towards Oneness: Acceptance

   - Embrace the process of letting go as a natural part of life.

   - Move towards a sense of unity with all.

5. Existential Aloneness: Embracing Solitude.

    -   Recognise solitude as a space for self-discovery.

    -   Build comfort with one's own inner world.

6. Sanatana Dharma: Timeless Principles

    -   Learn the essence of enduring spiritual principles.

    -   Apply these teachings to live a more conscious, meaningful life.

7. Spiritual Awakening: Transformation

    -   Experience a shift in consciousness and perspective.

    -   Embrace spiritual awakening as a path to deeper self-awareness.

Spiritual Growth (Chapters 13-18)

These chapters cover practices and philosophies that cultivate inner depth and spiritual understanding.

1. The Attitude of Gratitude: Cultivating Positivity

    -   Foster gratitude as a daily practice for uplifting the spirit.

    -   See gratitude as a gateway to abundance and peace.

2. Meditation: Mindfulness Practices

    -   Practice mindfulness to centre the mind and nurture peace.

    -   Use meditation as a tool for self-awareness and inner calm.

3. Nature of the Spirit: Exploring Essence

    -   Delve into the nature of spirit as a pure, eternal presence.

    -   Recognise your essence beyond material existence.

4. The Significance of Gayatri Mantra: Ancient Wisdom

    -   Appreciate the Gayatri Mantra as a timeless tool for enlightenment.

    -   Experience the mantra's ability to purify and elevate the mind.

5. Yoga: Union with Self

    -   Practice yoga as a means to harmonise body, mind, and spirit.

    -   Discover self-union as the ultimate aim of yoga.

6. Who is God? Exploring Divinity

    -   Contemplate divinity in personal and universal forms.

- Develop a personal connection with the divine, beyond labels.

Advanced Spirituality (Chapters 19-24)

This part explores complex themes and practices to deepen the spiritual journey.

1. Navigating Certainty to Uncertainty: Embracing Mystery.

    - Embrace the unknown as a space for growth and learning.

    - Find comfort in mystery, allowing life to unfold.

2. Our Conscience: Inner Guidance

    - Tune into the conscience as a compass for ethical living.

    - Honour inner guidance as a source of wisdom and truth.

3. Spirituality: Integrating Principles.

    - Synthesise spiritual principles into everyday life.

    - Live spirituality as a practice, not just a belief.

4. Prayer: Communicating with the Divine.

    - See prayer as a sacred dialogue with the divine.

- Use prayer to cultivate humility, love, and clarity.

5. The Purpose of Life: Discovering Meaning.

    - Reflect on life's deeper purpose and your unique role in it.

    - Align daily actions with a sense of higher purpose.

6. Spiritual Evolution: Growth Stages

    - Recognise the stages of spiritual growth as a continuous journey.

    - Accept each stage with patience and grace.

Practical Applications (Chapters 25-26)

These final chapters provide tools and reflections for sustaining spiritual progress in everyday life.

1. Spiritual Evolution and Energy Levels: Enhancing Vitality.

    - Recognise energy as a reflection of spiritual vitality.

    - Learn ways to cultivate and protect your spiritual energy.

2. The Power of Beliefs: Transformative Thinking.

    - Understand how beliefs shape perception and experience.

- Use empowering beliefs as a foundation for a fulfilling life.

Key Takeaways from Chapters 27 and 28

My Spiritual Experiences:

Spiritual experiences, like overcoming a cyclone with unwavering faith or the rain-soaked ascent to Sabarimala, illustrate life's storms as pathways to resilience, surrender, and divine connection. Each challenge becomes a metaphor for spiritual growth, cleansing distractions, and aligning with a higher purpose.

Spiritual Practices:

In daily life, practices such as meditation, gratitude, mindfulness, and acts of kindness nurture inner balance and clarity. Evening rituals like reflection, journaling, and candlelight meditation foster peace and self-awareness. Incorporating simplicity, digital detox, and solitude helps detach from materialism, paving the way for deeper introspection and spiritual fulfilment.

Sacred Beginings
Three Profound Cosmic Truths

Once upon a timeless realm, beyond the material universe, there were three beings known simply as Zero, One, and Infinity. Each of them represented a profound cosmic truth, and together, they wove the tapestry of existence.

The Void and the Awakening of One

In the beginning, there was Zero. Zero was the embodiment of the Void, a silent and serene nothingness. It was vast and boundless, yet empty, and held within it the infinite potential of all that could be. Zero was content in its silence, for it was aware of the peace that comes from embracing nothingness. But deep within the Void, there stirred a desire – a gentle ripple in the fabric of nothingness.

Life was born, and from this ripple emerged One.

One was the spark of creation, the first note in the grand symphony of existence. Where "Zero" was Formless (the spirit), One was Form. Where "Zero" was still, "One" was in motion. One stood in awe of Zero, recognising the vast potential it held.

But One also felt an urge to understand itself, to explore, to experience the fullness of being. And so, "One" danced through the Void, creating patterns, rhythms, and relationships.

The Quest for Infinity

As One danced, it felt the need for something greater, something beyond its individual experience. It began to sense Infinity, a presence that seemed both near and far. Infinity was the cosmic unity, the All-That-Is, and yet it was also beyond reach, a paradox of boundless expansion and unfathomable wholeness.

One yearned to merge with Infinity, to touch the entirety of existence. But Infinity was beyond a single form, beyond a single moment. Each time One thought it had reached Infinity, it realised there was more – a deeper level of understanding, a greater layer of reality.

The Lesson of Unity and the Return to the Source

One was frustrated, feeling as though Infinity was an endless horizon it could never quite reach. In this frustration, it returned to Zero and said, "Teach me your secret, for I have danced through the Void, yet I cannot grasp Infinity."

Zero, in its quiet wisdom, replied, "You see yourself as separate, and that is why you cannot reach Infinity. **Infinity is not something to be grasped, but something to become.** When you let go of being One, you become all that is. Infinity and Zero are two sides of the same truth."

With this revelation, one closed its eyes, surrendered its form, and dissolved back into the Void. In that moment, the boundaries faded, and One experienced itself as both Zero and Infinity – nothing and everything, the silent and the boundless.

The Infinite Dance

And so, Zero, One, and Infinity continued their cosmic dance, each giving rise to the other in a never-ending cycle. Zero was the beginning and the end, the eternal pause before the symphony and the final note that returns to silence. One was the journey, the spark of individual experience, the quest to know. And Infinity was the boundless whole, the union of all that was, is, and ever will be.

In the end, Zero, One, and Infinity were not separate beings at all. They were facets of the same timeless truth – the unity of nothingness and everything, of form and formlessness, of the finite and the infinite. And in that unity, they found peace, knowing that all paths ultimately return to the Source.

Zero is equal to infinity. Zero is powerful because it is infinity's twin.

$$0 = \infty$$

CHAPTER 1
BMI Chart

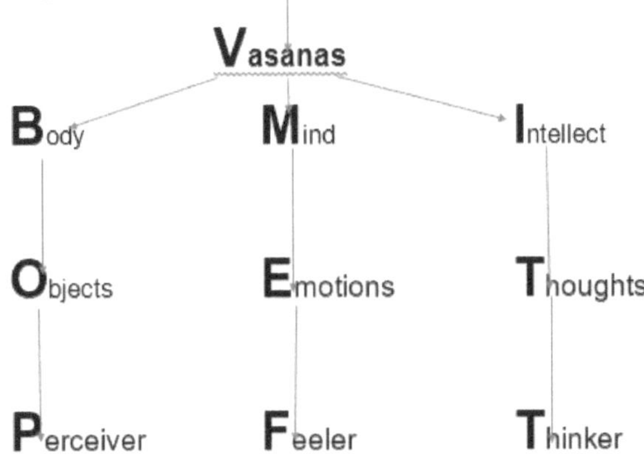

Swami Chinmayananda had devised this simple chart represented by 11 letters to understand about ourselves and the world that we live in. How we can get harmony through the vehicles (the B, M, I) in the world of (O, E, T).

1. OM represents Consciousness, Reality, or God

2. V represents Vasanas: Impressions in the subconscious mind

3. **B, M, I are the Equipment: Body, Mind, and Intellect**

4. **O, E, T are the fields of experiences: Objects and Emotions, Thoughts.**

5. **P, F, T are the individualised ego. Perceiver, Feeler, and Thinker.**

When Consciousness expresses itself through the equipment, the body, via the senses on the world of Objects, one becomes a Perceiver.

When Consciousness expresses itself through the mind in the field of emotions, one becomes a Feeler.

When Consciousness expresses itself through the intellect in the field of thoughts, one becomes a Thinker.

The Perceiver, the Feeler, and the Thinker are the individualised ego.

The human body encompasses not only the physical senses but also the mind with its range of emotions, instincts, and impulses, as well as the intellect with its capacity for rational thought—all of which are ultimately composed of matter. Physically, the body is made up of elements like carbon, calcium, and phosphorus. The denser aspects of matter make up the gross physical body, while subtler forms contribute to the mind and intellect. Regardless of whether matter is gross or subtle, it remains inert and lifeless. Yet, humans are conscious and dynamic. This raises an essential question: from where does this consciousness arise?

Consider a car and its various parts, all made of inert matter. Despite this, a car can move. What gives it the power to do so? Similarly, when a bulb lights up, there must be something beyond the bulb itself expressing through it. Likewise, something beyond the body and its faculties enables it to function. When this "something" ceases to express, the body lies inactive; emotions, thoughts, and faculties no longer operate. Life itself has stopped flowing through it.

This points to the need for something "beyond matter"—the Body, Mind, and Intellect (BMI)—to animate these faculties. Ancient texts, such as the Bible, reference this as God's presence within all beings, sustaining and empowering each individual by divine grace. Just as a bulb shines due to the presence of electricity, humans live and function through the presence of a force beyond physical matter. This vital force, other than matter, is known as the spirit. It represents a unified consciousness, or spark of existence, which is singular, though it manifests uniquely in everyone.

This consciousness is symbolised by the sound "Aum." When this consciousness channels through the sense organs—eyes, ears, nose, tongue, and skin—it gives rise to a sense of individual identity: the "I" who perceives through these senses. Each experience—seeing, hearing, smelling, tasting, and touching—is not simply a bodily function; "it is the expression of consciousness through the senses." The eyes, for instance, cannot see on their own; consciousness must operate through them. A transplanted eye continues to function not because of its structure alone, but due to the consciousness of its new host.

We often say, "I see," "I hear," "I smell," but this means we are aware of these actions; it is the consciousness behind the senses that makes these experiences possible. This awareness through the senses transforms us into perceivers of the world around us. Similarly, when consciousness flows through the mind, we become feelers, experiencing emotions like love, jealousy, and passion. When it flows through the intellect, we become thinkers, engaging in rational thought and reflection. Thus, the fields of objects, emotions, and thoughts represent realms from which we derive experiences through the BMI.

The BMI serves as the tools through which one engages with life, while the fields of objects, emotions, and thoughts (OET) are the settings for these experiences. Meanwhile, the individualised ego, or "I," emerges as the Perceiver, Feeler, and Thinker (PFT) through the varied lenses of body, mind, and intellect. Recognising that "I" see through the eyes, rather than with them, fosters a sense of inner independence.

In this understanding, Consciousness—the true "I"—becomes the seer in the eyes, the hearer in the ears, the feeler in the mind, and the thinker in the intellect. However, when one forgets this true identity and instead identifies with the body, mind, and intellect, suffering arises. By realising that one is the Consciousness, distinct from the limited ego (the "i" that perceives, feels, and thinks), it becomes possible to transcend life's sorrows. This shift in understanding allows one to engage with life from a place of greater clarity and peace.

What Are Vasanas?

Vasanas are a key concept in Vedantic philosophy, but they lack a direct English equivalent. The closest term to describe Vasanas is unmanifested desires – latent tendencies or inclinations that do not actively express themselves but exist in a potential state.

To illustrate, imagine an artist deeply passionate about painting. During the day, he channels his love for art into creating paintings. However, when he goes to sleep, his active engagement with art ceases. Yet, when he wakes up the next morning, he resumes being an artist, driven by the same love for painting. He does not suddenly wake up as a philosopher or a scientist. This continuity suggests that his love for art, though dormant during sleep, still existed in a latent state. This latent state of desires during deep sleep is what we call Vasanas.

Vasanas form the root of all aspects of our personality and actions. They manifest into desires, which lead to thoughts, actions, and eventually shape our environment. For example, if you have a vasana for philosophy, it might prompt a thought to explore it further, which then becomes the desire to listen to a philosophical lecture. This desire transforms into action as you attend the lecture, creating an environment conducive to philosophical learning.

Vasanas and the Causal Body:

Vasanas are deeply connected to what Vedanta refers to as the causal body – the fundamental cause behind our intellect, thoughts, emotions, actions, and surroundings. When in deep sleep, where no thoughts or desires manifest, we experience a state of relative calm or bliss. This is referred to as the anandamaya kosha or the bliss sheath. It is called so because in this state, the mind is free from the disturbances of manifest desires.

Vasanas as Avidya (Ignorance).

Vasanas are also synonymous with avidya, which means ignorance of the true self. This ignorance gives rise to our sense of individuality and our perception of the world. When one attains self-knowledge, this ignorance dissolves, along with the personality and world it creates.

The Inconceivable Nature of Vasanas

Despite numerous attempts to define Vasanas, they remain beyond the grasp of the human intellect. They are the very source of the intellect and thus cannot be fully comprehended by it. Vasanas are inconceivable; we cannot directly know them but only recognise their manifestations as thoughts, desires, or actions.

In summary, while Vasanas can be described as unmanifested desires, they are ultimately beyond intellectual definition. They are the subtle undercurrent shaping our lives, yet they lie outside the realm of direct understanding.

Vasana is the veil between the individual and God.

CHAPTER 2

The Journey to Self-Discovery – Exploring One's True Nature – "Nothing-ness"

RKN Mangal was a billionaire in the pharmaceutical industry, yet despite his wealth, he felt deeply unfulfilled. Friends advised him to learn meditation from a true master, believing it could bring him inner peace. After seeking recommendations, his closest aide informed him that Sage Rama, who lived in the Shivani mountains of the Himalayas, was considered the best teacher. Sage Rama was known for his constant communion with a higher power.

Mangal decided to make the journey, accompanied by a dozen well-dressed men in suits, ties, and polished shoes. He too dressed in his finest attire, reflecting his status. With much pomp, the group arrived at the sage's humble and tranquil hut, where Sage Rama sat peacefully, his eyes closed in deep meditation, a serene smile on his face, unaware of the bustling activity around him.

The sound of leaves rustling and the whispers of the men disturbed the sage's meditation. Slowly, he opened his eyes and saw the group before him. Mangal stepped forward, bowed respectfully, and greeted the sage with a "Namaste."

Sage Rama looked at him and asked, "What do you want?"

Mangal replied, "I want to learn meditation. People say you are the best teacher."

The sage then asked, "Who are you?"

Surprised, Mangal responded, "Don't you know? I am RKN Mangal."

The sage said calmly, "That's your name. Tell me who you are."

Mangal, a bit perplexed, replied, "I'm from ZEE Pharmaceuticals."

"That's your company's name. Tell me who you are," the sage repeated.

Mangal continued, "I am the Managing Director of the company."

"That's your job title. Tell me who you are," the sage asked again.

Frustrated, Mangal said, "Are you joking? Our company is on the Fortune 500 list."

"That's your company's status. Tell me who you are," the sage persisted.

Mangal, feeling cornered, said, "I graduated first from Stanford with an MBA."

"That's your education. Tell me who you are."

Mangal, now sweating, added, "My father founded the company from scratch in 1980."

"That's about your father. Who are you?" the sage asked once more.

"My son Deepak is the CEO of the company now," Mangal said, struggling.

The sage smiled and said, "I didn't ask about your son or descendants. I'm asking you: Who are you?"

With 11 pairs of eyes on him, Mangal, overwhelmed and confused, finally replied, "Master, I give up. I don't know who I am. I guess I am actually 'nothing'."

The sage smiled warmly and said, "Now, that's a good place to begin. Let's begin!"

The concept "We are all nothing" can be a powerful and liberating attitude. Here's an elaboration:

Acknowledging that our individual existence, accomplishments, and possessions are temporary and insignificant in the grand scheme.

Implications:

1. Humility: Recognise the fleeting nature of life and ego.

2. Interconnectedness: Understand that we're part of a larger whole.

3. Non-attachment: Let go of attachment to possessions, status, and outcomes.

4. Gratitude: Appreciate the present moment and its simple joys.

5. Freedom: Release the burden of self-importance and expectations.

Benefits:

1. Reduced stress and anxiety.

2. Increased empathy and compassion.

3. Greater sense of unity and cooperation.

4. Improved mental clarity and focus.

5. Enhanced creativity and openness.

Quotes:

1. "The only true wisdom is in knowing you know nothing." - Socrates.

2. "Emptiness is not nothing, but the very essence of being." - Bodhidharma.

3. "The smaller we make ourselves, the greater we become." - Rabindranath Tagore.

In discovering that we are nothing, we become everything!

CHAPTER 3
Happiness is Always Inside

The statement "Happiness is in the being; success is in the becoming" carries deep wisdom. Many believe that greater success will lead to greater happiness, yet success often brings only fleeting joy, not lasting contentment. No matter what we achieve, there's always something that can disturb our happiness. We might think, "I'll be happy if I get another car, a bigger house, a higher salary, a promotion, a big bonus," and so on. But would achieving all these desires truly make us happy? The answer is often no.

True happiness can be experienced right here, right now, if we adopt the right mindset. Happiness is an attitude, a choice. Choosing to be happy regardless of circumstances is the approach of a wise person. It's easier said than done! Many believe happiness lies outside of them, something to be acquired or found. But happiness is, in fact, within us – it's a state we can cultivate. When we constantly think, "I'll be happy when I go abroad, become a GM, buy a luxury watch..." we end up postponing our happiness endlessly.

True happiness isn't found in future achievements; it's discovered by embracing the present moment and cultivating a mindset of contentment, regardless of external conditions.

There's a story in the Upanishads about the Kasturi Mriga, or musk deer, which serves as a beautiful metaphor for the search for happiness and the divine. It reminds us that while we often seek God and fulfilment outside of ourselves, they have always been within us.

As the story goes, one day, a musk deer caught a whiff of a captivating, aromatic scent. Intrigued and entranced by the fragrance, the deer began a relentless search, roaming the forest, driven by an unshakeable desire to find its source. No matter the obstacles or dangers, it pressed on, braving harsh weather and rugged terrain.

After days of tireless wandering, the deer, exhausted and wounded from a fall off a cliff, lay on the ground. In its final moments, it realised with a sense of profound irony that the musk had been within it all along, emanating from its own body.

This story teaches us that the peace and divinity we seek are not distant or hidden – they are within us, waiting to be discovered. Just as the deer spent its life searching outward, we often look outside ourselves for happiness, unaware that the true source of joy and connection with the divine lies within.

CHAPTER 4
FAITH: The Invisible Connection with the Creator

Belief is when you accept an idea regardless of it being logical or illogical. Belief comes after reasoning and argument, and it can be changed when there is doubt in one's mind. But Trust and Faith are even closer. Trust has memory, Faith doesn't. Trust is intelligent, Faith is innocent. Trust comes after Love, Faith brings love. Trust observes, Faith believes. FAITH = BELIEF + ACTION + CONFIDENCE.

One of the most important spiritual qualities that one needs to cultivate is FAITH. Faith is the one true source of support on which we can always rely in the rough and tough journey called Life upon this earth. Faith is a knowledge within the heart beyond the reach of proof, said Kahlil Gibran. It means complete trust or confidence in someone or something, and in the spiritual context, it means faith in God or in the doctrines or teachings of religion.

Some real-time examples of people who had faith...

1. Inspired by my friend Captain K.K. Venkatraman who was with the Kumaon Regiment (6th Battalion) during the Indo-Pak war (Liberation of East Pakistan and creation of Bangladesh) in 1971 and who narrated his spiritual experience of doing the Narmada Parikrama (circumambulation/Pradakshinam) all by himself in the year 1987 covering a distance of 2620 km by foot, I am writing this article on "FAITH." While "Girivalam" (going round a hill) is common, going round a river is uncommon. In fact, there are only two rivers associated with this practice. People go round Ganga for a short stretch from Rishikesh to Haridwar using the bridges at these places. But Narmada is the only river people walk round the entire length (generally clockwise) on barefoot without carrying money and surviving only on sought or offered food. This parikrama is normally done by villagers living in the valley in 3 years, 3 months, and 13 days. Captain Venkatraman did it in 131 days!

    Narmada is the longest of the west-flowing rivers of India. The river originates from a holy tank in Amarkantak in M.P., situated 1050 m above sea level. The landscapes along the meandering Narmada are thickly forested slopes, rocky regions with falls, and cultivated lands. The 2528 km journey walking round the river (covering both banks) is difficult because one has to do it barefoot through rough terrain, forests which are the habitat for wild animals, snakes, and to live only on bhiksha observing severe austerities, without carrying money. One should observe a vow of chastity, sleep on the floor, should not shave or cut hair, not use oil, soap, and walk only from sunrise to sunset. Captain Venkatraman started his Parikrama on 26th October 1987 and completed it on 4th March 1988, walking a distance of 2528 km in 131 days, about 20 km/day!!

Having confidence in himself, FAITH in the supreme Grace (this task would have otherwise been impossible), and the physical toughness and mental robustness acquired during his Army service, he courageously undertook this arduous task. Regular practice of Suryanamaskar, Yogasana, and Pranayama for years helped him in keeping his mind effortlessly under control and vision focused on the goal.

He says nothing is impossible if one has confidence in oneself, unshakeable faith in the Almighty, and adds that a man of FAITH lives in Peace, with Stability, and equanimity. Faith is taking the first step even if you don't see the full staircase!! Walking cross country, the ankles of Captain did not get twisted even once, nor did he step on a snake!! His weight remained almost the same after his Narmada Parikrama. In fact, he did not carry any money but had deep faith in God who would provide him food, and the villagers fed him generously. Only on two occasions did he not get food during the entire 131 days!! Captain accepts that it was because of his ego!!

2. The American effort to send astronauts to the moon has its origins in a famous appeal President John F. Kennedy made to a special joint session of Congress on May 25, 1961. I believe with great faith that this nation should commit itself to achieving this goal before this decade is out, of landing a man on the moon and returning him safely to earth. From belief to reason, through reason to knowledge, from knowledge to action with confidence to ultimate faith, Apollo 11 landed on the moon after covering a distance of around 400,000 kilometres and Neil Armstrong and Edwin Aldrin Jr set their foot on the moon.

3. Dr Mark is a cancer specialist in the U.S. He had set off on a long flight to participate in a conference and receive an award for his contribution in the field of medical research. He boarded the flight and 2 hours after the flight took off, it had to land on an emergency basis since the aircraft had developed a technical snag. On alighting from the aircraft, Dr Mark went to the counter and tried to get a ticket on the next immediate aircraft but was dismayed to hear that the next flight was at least 8 hours away; he was certain that he would not make it to the conference. The girl at the reception, however, told him that if he could rent a car, he could drive the distance to his destination in 4 hours. Frantically, he rented the car and started driving towards the conference city at a full clip. It was certainly not his day, he thought, for suddenly the weather changed and a heavy thunderstorm.

The heavy downpour made it very difficult to stay on track, yet keep up the speed. Halfway through, he missed a turn and was proceeding fast in the wrong direction. The weather grew worse, and he realised that he had lost his way; the lights were receding, and the road was deserted. He was searching for some habitation, and he was happy when he saw an old dilapidated house. He parked his car in the front, and with the rains pouring, he crossed the road and reached the house completely wet. A young lady opened the door, and Mark asked her if he could use her telephone. The lady replied that she did not have a phone but requested him to come inside, dry himself, have some tea, and something to eat before the weather cleared. Exhausted, Dr Mark stepped inside gratefully and accepted her offer. The lady then asked if he could join in for prayers. Dr Mark smiled and said, "I don't believe in prayers, but believe in only hard work;" however, he requested her to go about with her prayers.

Sipping his tea, he saw through the dim lights that the lady was sitting near a baby crib praying. Every time she finished her prayer, she would continue with another one. Dr. Mark sensed that the lady needed some help from God and that's why she was praying. Once the lady was through with her prayers, Dr. Mark asked her, "If I may ask you, what exactly are you praying to God? And who is the child in the crib?" The lady replied, "It's a sad story, sir." The child in the crib is my son, and he is suffering from a rare type of cancer." Mark said, "So why don't you have him treated by a specialist?" The lady replied, "I am told that for this particular type of cancer, only Dr. Mark can cure, and I can't afford the fees, and moreover, he lives in a faraway city." The lady continued, "But sir, God will definitely create a way one day, and my son will definitely get cured; I will not allow my fears to quell the faith I have in God. Sooner or later, God will help me."

Stunned and overwhelmed, he fell on his knees and started crying. He said, all along he was neither a Theist nor an Atheist nor an Agnostic but believed only in hard work. He spoke in a quiet voice and told her about the sequence of events that took place earlier during the day – malfunctioning in the plane, a thunderstorm hit, and how he lost his way and finally her prayers. He declared, "All this happened for God to not only answer your prayers but also for people who live in this materialistic world and give some time to the hapless people who do not have many resources but rich prayer and devotion to be helped." The storm did clear and the three of them went to the city where Dr. Mark lived, the surgery was performed, and after a few months everything became alright for the lady and her son.

Faith works... Miracles do happen... Faith without works is dead. Faith is seeing with the eyes of the heart. It has been said that faith sees the invisible, believes the incredible, and receives the impossible. Faith and fear do not exist together, nor do faith and doubt exist together. Faith also means confidence, belief, loyalty, or allegiance. To one who has faith, no explanation is necessary. To one without faith, no explanation is possible, said St. Thomas of Aquinas.

The life of man is powered by faith. We repose our faith in our parents when we are young. As we grow older, friends, family, spouses, partners are added to the list of people we trust. We have faith in the law of the land, in the system of justice and governance, we have faith in medicine, doctors, engineers. Life cannot pose a question which faith cannot answer... Faith is the key to the Universe. Faith does not, however, guarantee that we will never come face to face with sorrow, suffering, weakness, or disappointment. But faith can give us the courage, the right attitude, and ability to face the problems and emerge victorious. Faith in God and in one's own self is a virtue.

Doubt is sin. Faith is like Wi-Fi, it's invisible but has the power to connect you to what you need. Jesus said, "Truly I tell you if you have faith as small as a mustard seed, you can say to this mountain, 'Move from here to there,' and it will move. Nothing will be impossible for you. Faith is the transference of responsibility and understanding that it is not my will but thy will which would prevail. God sometimes upsets your plans so that he could execute His and His plans are always right. Faith is the invisible connecting link between you and the Creator of the design of the Universe.

Faith works... if you have faith!!

CHAPTER 5
Finding Tranquillity Amidst Chaos: Maintaining Inner Peace

We often talk about tranquillity, but it's not just about being in a quiet, peaceful place like a retreat, a hill station, or a cosy resort, or even a walk in the woods. Those are external sources of calm. While we may visit such places occasionally, the reality is that most of us spend our time in noisy environments—markets, offices, hospitals, or courts—where the external noise can be overwhelming.

True tranquillity, however, comes from within. It requires a calm heart and the ability to concentrate on what truly matters, no matter the external circumstances. To achieve this, we must focus on the task at hand, ignoring distractions.

One effective way to maintain focus is by listing your tasks—on paper or digitally—and prioritising them. Take on one task at a time, and even when multitasking is necessary, deeply focus on one task before moving to the next.

Here's a story to reflect on:

Once upon a time, a young disciple seeking enlightenment set out on a journey to visit a famous Zen Master, renowned for his wisdom. After travelling for days, crossing mountains and valleys, the disciple finally arrived at the simple home of the master. Filled with anticipation, he approached and said, "Master, please teach me the secret to finding inner peace and tranquillity."

The Zen Master smiled warmly and gestured for the disciple to follow him. They walked together in silence until they reached a small teahouse in the heart of a bustling marketplace. As they entered, the disciple became acutely aware of the surrounding chaos – merchants shouting, customers haggling, and the general clamour of a busy market.

Without a word, the Zen Master sat down at a table and motioned for the disciple to join him. A server came over and asked, "What can I get for you?" The master simply replied, "Two cups of tea, please."

As they waited, the disciple found himself overwhelmed by the noise. Unable to contain his frustration, he turned to the master and asked, "Master, how can anyone find peace in the midst of all this chaos? The noise is unbearable."

The Zen Master smiled gently and asked, "Tell me, what do you hear?"

The disciple listened and replied, "I hear the merchants shouting, customers bargaining, and the clatter of dishes."

The master nodded. "And what do you see?"

The disciple looked around. "People rushing, colourful goods everywhere, and the busyness of the marketplace."

The Zen Master smiled again and said, "Now, focus on our table. What do you hear?"

The disciple turned his attention to their immediate surroundings, listening closely. To his surprise, the noise of the marketplace seemed to fade. "Master, I can only hear the tea being prepared. The noise from outside has disappeared,"

The Zen Master nodded approvingly. "You see, my dear disciple, this is **the power of ignoring**. When you focus on what truly matters and let go of unnecessary distractions, you create your own peace. The noise of the world will always be there, but it's up to you to choose what enters your mind and heart."

The disciple's eyes widened with understanding. He realised that peace wasn't about silencing the world, but about changing his own focus. From that moment, he understood that inner peace comes not from changing the outside world, but from changing his perception and where he places his attention.

Grateful for the wisdom he had received, the disciple continued his journey, learning to ignore the noise of the world and cultivate inner peace. He carried with him the master's lesson: that the power of ignoring is not about turning a blind eye to life, but about consciously choosing where to direct one's thoughts and energy. By focusing on what truly matters, one can find peace and clarity, even amidst chaos. He kept a placard on his table which read, **"Think what you want to think."**

We should strive to ignore the distractions presented by the outside world that come in leaps and bounds.

CHAPTER 6

Transcending Ego (Letting Go of Ego Boundaries)

When we were in the mother's womb, we were in a deep state of meditation. When we were born, the senses came into the picture. We had three equipment: The body, the mind, and the Intellect. We started having our individuality, the sense of (i) the limited ego which started differentiating, comparing, dividing, not knowing that it is part of the Whole. In Sanskrit, this limited individuality is called the Jivatma, and the Ultimate Reality is called Paramatma. Through spiritual practices, one could transcend the levels of Consciousness to finally merge into the Whole.

Ego, or Ahamkara in Sanskrit, refers to the identification with one's individual self, creating a sense of separation and distinction from others and the universe.

Characteristics of Ego:

1. Separation: Seeing oneself as distinct from others and the universe.

2. Identification: Associating with thoughts, emotions, and experiences.

3. Ownership: Believing "I" am the doer, owner, or controller.

4. Comparison: Measuring oneself against others.

5. Attachment: Clinging to desires, possessions, and outcomes.

Here are three stories illustrating ego transcendence:

Story 1: The Story of Ramana Maharshi and His Mother

Ramana Maharshi, a renowned Indian sage, was known for his profound self-inquiry and ego-transcending wisdom. A pivotal event in his life illustrates the power of ego transcendence:

After Ramana's spiritual awakening at age 16, he left home to pursue his spiritual quest. His mother, Azhagammal, was devastated by his departure. She searched for him, finally finding him at the holy hill of Arunachala.

Initially, Ramana's mother tried to persuade him to return home, but he refused. Feeling rejected, she began to live near him, serving him, and eventually becoming his devotee.

One day, while caring for Ramana, his mother grew attached to her role and started to feel possessive about her son's attention. Ramana recognised her ego-identification and decided to teach her a lesson.

He stopped responding to her, ignoring her presence. Azhagammal felt hurt, confused, and eventually realised her attachment was ego-driven. She surrendered, letting go of her possessiveness.

Ramana then shared a profound insight:

"The ego is like a cloth wrapped around the lamp, hiding its light. Remove the cloth, and the light shines brightly. Similarly, transcend the ego, and the Self shines forth."

Azhagammal's ego transcendence transformed her relationship with Ramana. **She no longer saw him as her son but as the divine itself. Her love became selfless, and she served him with detachment.**

Story 2: The Humble Potter

A skilled potter, renowned for exquisite ceramics, lived in ancient India. His ego grew with fame. One day, while travelling, he met a wise sage.

The sage asked, "Who creates your masterpieces?"

The potter proudly replied, "I do."

The sage smiled, handed him clay, and asked, "Create something without your hands."

Perplexed, the potter prayed, surrendering ego. Guided by intuition, his feet shaped a flawless vase.

The sage said, "You didn't create; the universe flowed through you. Transcend ego, and true mastery emerges."

Story 3: The River's Lesson

A swollen river, bursting with pride, boasted to the ocean, "I'm mighty, powerful!"

The ocean calmly replied, "Your strength lies not in turbulence, but flow. Surrender, merge with me, and become limitless."

The river's ego dissolved as it merged, transforming into a serene, life-giving force.

Some real-life inspiring stories of transcending ego:

Historical Figures:

1. Nelson Mandela: After 27 years in prison, Mandela chose forgiveness over resentment, demonstrating remarkable humility.

2. Mahatma Gandhi: Renounced wealth and status to lead India's non-violent independence movement.

Everyday Heroes:

1. The Anonymous Donor: A wealthy businessman donated millions anonymously, humbly attributing success to community support.

2. The Selfless Volunteer: A young professional dedicated her life to disaster relief, putting others' needs before her own.

Personal Transformations:

1. Rick Hansen: Paralysed athlete transformed into advocate, raising millions for spinal cord research.

2. Malala Yousafzai: Surviving assassination attempts, Malala continued advocating for education, prioritising purpose over personal safety.

Business Leaders:

1. Howard Schultz (Starbucks): Stepped down as CEO, acknowledging limitations and returned to lead company transformation.

2. Richard Branson (Virgin Group): Empowers employees, fostering collaborative leadership.

Sports Icons:

1. Mohammad Ali: Boxing legend's humility and philanthropy overshadowed boastful persona.

2. LeBron James: NBA star prioritizes community development, education, and social justice.

Transcending the ego is a form of transformation. Just as life emerges when an egg opens from within, personal growth follows a similar process. To achieve this, one must first acknowledge the presence of the ego. Practising self-awareness, embracing humility, and fostering gratitude are essential steps on this journey. **Take off the E and let it GO!**

CHAPTER 7
Internal versus External Power: Shakthi and Durga

In Hinduism, the word Durga represents external power, symbolising the strength found in technology, law, social status, wealth, property, organisational roles, and social standing. The term "Durg" means fortress, reflecting the protective structures early humans developed to shield themselves from predators. Initially, these fences were simple, made of straw, evolving over time into wooden, bamboo, mud, stone, and finally stone-and-brick fortifications.

Durga is often depicted riding a lion—the king of the jungle—a symbol of strength, courage, royalty, power, aggression, and fierceness. This portrayal resonates with leaders who seek to emulate these qualities, using external power to dominate, subdue, and manage others, often to reinforce their own sense of security and significance. Such displays of authority and status, like wealth or hierarchy, are manifestations of "Durga-ness."

While Durga can be summoned or relinquished through rituals like Yajna (sacrifice), Shakthi—the internal, enduring power—cannot be given or taken externally. Shakthi arises from tapas (austerity and discipline) and embodies intrinsic qualities like resilience, motivation, drive, and patience. Too much focus on external Durga often compensates for a lack of Shakthi; however, as one cultivates Shakthi, the need for external displays of power diminishes.

Modern materialists and activists often prioritise Durga over Shakthi, whereas spiritualists and counsellors value Shakthi. Spiritual practitioners focus on empowering the self, encouraging individuals to cultivate inner strength, personal responsibility, and autonomy rather than relying on external validation or control. Those who nurture Shakthi experience reduced anxiety and insecurity, outgrowing the reactive, "animal" instincts within.

This distinction between Shakthi and Durga—internal versus external power—offers a nuanced understanding of power from an Indian perspective. The goal is to transcend base impulses, empowering ourselves and others through our inner Shakthi.

CHAPTER 8

The Four Pillars of Spiritual Growth in *At the Feet of the Master*

At the Feet of the Master, written under the name of J. Krishnamurti (though he is credited there as Alcyone), is a compact but profound guide on the essentials of spiritual life. The book, written in a direct, accessible style, emphasises four cardinal virtues essential to spiritual growth and inner understanding: Discrimination, Desire-lessness, Good Conduct, and Love. Each of these principles aims to guide the spiritual aspirant in finding deeper truths and living in alignment with inner wisdom.

1. Discrimination

Discrimination, or discernment, is the ability to distinguish between the real and the unreal, the temporary and the eternal. Krishnamurti emphasises the importance of recognising what is truly valuable in life. According to him, spiritual seekers often become entangled in superficial desires and distractions, which ultimately divert them from their true purpose. Discrimination helps one distinguish between what is essential for spiritual growth and what merely satisfies transient desires.

To cultivate discrimination, he advises the aspirant to look beyond sensory experiences and transient pleasures, which are often misleading. Instead, seekers should train themselves to focus on the eternal – the qualities and values that endure beyond the physical and temporary. This principle calls for clarity of mind and purpose, which Krishnamurti suggests can only come through introspection, self-inquiry, and sincere dedication to truth.

2. Desire-lessness

Desire-lessness is the detachment from worldly desires and attachments, which bind us to material life and prevent us from realising our higher self. According to Krishnamurti, most desires are grounded in the ego and therefore serve to reinforce a false sense of identity, creating suffering. This does not mean one should reject all possessions or relationships, but rather that one should cultivate an inner freedom, where attachments do not control or define one's life.

In Krishnamurti's view, true freedom comes from letting go of the "I" and "mine" mentality. For the aspirant, this includes renouncing the fruits of actions and instead performing duties selflessly. By cultivating this state of detachment, one remains unperturbed by both pleasure and pain. He notes that the mind should be like still water, undisturbed by waves of desire, achieving peace and calm that allow the seeker to act with a pure and focused intention.

3. Good Conduct

Good conduct is the manifestation of ethical and moral values that align with a life of integrity and service. Krishnamurti's framework for good conduct includes several essential qualities:

Self-control: Mastery over one's mind and emotions to ensure one's actions are wise and not impulsive.

Tolerance: The openness to accept and understand others' perspectives, even when they differ from one's own.

Cheerfulness: A light-hearted, positive attitude, which not only enriches one's own life but uplifts those around them.

Unselfishness: Acting without a selfish motive, thinking of others' well-being, and being of service to humanity.

Krishnamurti insists that good conduct is not only about moral correctness but also about the sincerity and authenticity behind one's actions. Each action, he argues, should stem from a place of love and truth rather than obligation or fear. A commitment to these virtues refines the soul and prepares it for higher wisdom.

4. Love

The fourth and most profound principle is love, which he describes as the very essence of life and the driving force behind all existence. Krishnamurti's notion of love transcends personal attachment or affection. It is universal love, an unbounded compassion that includes all beings without discrimination. Love, in this sense, is more than an emotion – it is a state of being, a deep recognition of the interconnectedness of all life.

To truly love, according to Krishnamurti, is to live without barriers of self-interest or prejudice. Such love naturally leads to humility, compassion, and the desire to alleviate the suffering of others. This love does not expect or demand anything in return, and it guides the seeker in transcending personal desires. Krishnamurti emphasises that only through love can one realise unity with the Divine, for it is love that dissolves the separation between self and other, between individual and universal.

The Path of Discipleship

Throughout *At the Feet of the Master*, Krishnamurti underscores that these four principles are not just theoretical ideals but practical aspects of spiritual discipline. He describes how living by these virtues is essential to the path of discipleship, where the aspirant seeks to be a true instrument of the Divine will. Discipleship, he explains, is about aligning oneself with the higher purpose and dedicating one's life to the service of humanity, guided by the light of truth.

For Krishnamurti, discipleship is an inner journey that requires dedication, self-discipline, and sincerity. The disciple must be vigilant, constantly observing the mind and striving for purity in thought, word, and deed. The ultimate goal is liberation from egoic attachments and the awakening of an inner consciousness that is rooted in love, truth, and wisdom.

The Inner and Outer Worlds

Krishnamurti frequently returns to the idea that the outer world is a reflection of the inner state. By purifying the inner world—one's thoughts, emotions, and intentions—one naturally transforms the outer world. This aligns with the mystical understanding that reality is shaped by consciousness, and that individual transformation is the foundation for social and global harmony.

Practical Application of the Principles

At the Feet of the Master serves not only as a guide for personal transformation but also as a practical manual for daily living. Krishnamurti emphasises that true wisdom lies in applying these principles, even in mundane activities. For instance, discrimination may be practiced when making choices about lifestyle and relationships, while Desire-lessness can be cultivated through mindful detachment from material objects and outcomes.

Good conduct, too, should be evident in everyday interactions—with friends, family, colleagues, and even strangers. Each moment, Krishnamurti suggests, is an opportunity to embody the highest virtues and bring one's life into alignment with spiritual ideals.

Conclusion

At the Feet of the Master encapsulates timeless wisdom, urging seekers to realise their highest potential by cultivating inner virtues. It is a call to live consciously, to act selflessly, and to love unconditionally. Krishnamurti's teachings are an invitation to transcend ego, find inner peace, and embrace life as an opportunity to serve the greater good.

In essence, the book is a guide to living a life of purpose and integrity, rooted in truth and love. Through Discrimination, Desire-lessness, Good Conduct, and Love, Krishnamurti offers a pathway for seekers to experience spiritual awakening and to contribute positively to the world. This journey, he reminds us, requires courage, patience, and unwavering sincerity but promises the joy and fulfilment of discovering the Divine within.

CHAPTER 9

Daily Loss: Moving Towards Oneness

From Zero to one to infinity is material; From Infinity to one is spiritual. Reflect on this story:

The king of a vast empire had heard of Sage Kapila's extraordinary wisdom and decided to seek his guidance, hoping it would help him govern effectively. The sage lived deep in a jungle on the Western Ghats, where the path to his hermitage was so dense that few had managed to reach it, and many who tried never returned.

Determined, the king set out with his ministers. After three days of navigating the wilderness, they lost their way. While they were wondering which direction to take, they encountered a young boy grazing a horse. Surprised to find anyone in such an isolated place, the king asked the boy if he knew where Sage Kapila resided. The boy nodded confidently, and something in his calm demeanour suggested he held knowledge beyond mere directions. Intrigued, the king began questioning the boy about his life, interests, and the place he called home.

The boy answered each question with clarity and insight beyond his years. Half-jokingly, the king asked, "Son, you seem to know so much for your age. Do you also know how to rule an empire?" The boy paused, considering the question, and replied, "I don't know much, sir, but perhaps managing an empire is a bit like managing my horse."

Curious, the king pressed, "How so?"

The boy explained, "With my horse, I only ensure nothing harmful touches it so it can thrive naturally. Perhaps managing an empire is similar—protect it from harm, and it will flourish on its own."

The simplicity and depth of the boy's words astonished the king and his ministers. The king dismounted, embraced the boy, and said, "You've given me the clarity I needed. When you feel ready, come see me—I am the king." He then turned to his ministers, who asked if they would still like to visit the sage. The king replied, "I have already found the answer I sought."

Just as the king realised his own approach to ruling could be simplified, we, too, can learn to simplify our lives by removing unnecessary complexities. The king's doubt in his rule led him to seek wisdom from a sage, just as we often look to spiritual guides for holistic solutions. Problems are fragmented, but solutions often arise from simplicity. By focusing on essentials, we can enhance vitality in all aspects of life.

Here are a few principles to reduce life's complexities:

- Streamline your thoughts: Focus on the vital few and let go of trivial distractions.

- Limit screen time: Spend less time on social media and more time connecting with those who truly matter.

- Avoid bad habits: Moderation is key – too much of anything can be harmful.

- Steer clear of negativity: Keep away from people and influences that weigh you down.

- Declutter: Clear physical clutter from your surroundings and mental clutter from your mind.

Set aside a few minutes each day for introspection. You'll start to notice where time is wasted and what habits steal energy. Let go of items you no longer use or need, and make a habit of removing one clutter from your life every day—a practice of "Daily Loss." Remove the un-essentials - from your life - one at a time.

CHAPTER 10
Existential Aloneness: Embracing Solitude

Though "aloneness" and "loneliness" are often used interchangeably, they hold different meanings, particularly from emotional and spiritual viewpoints.

Aloneness

Aloneness is the state of being physically by oneself, but without any negative emotional weight. It's a chosen or accepted state, fostering self-contentment and inner peace. In aloneness, you feel complete and whole, embracing a space for self-discovery, creativity, and spiritual growth. This solitude empowers you to connect more meaningfully with yourself and the world. People who embrace aloneness often engage in solitary activities like meditation, reflection, or personal hobbies. For them, solitude is rejuvenating and inwardly connecting, leading to self-sufficiency and profound inner freedom, where fulfilment comes from within, not from others.

Loneliness

Loneliness, in contrast, is an emotional state marked by feelings of isolation and a longing for connection. It arises from a perceived gap between desired relationships and actual ones, making one feel misunderstood or disconnected—even in the company of others. Loneliness is often accompanied by sadness, emptiness, and a yearning to fill an inner void. Unlike aloneness, which can be positive, loneliness is distressing and can harm well-being, leading to depression, anxiety, and a sense of hopelessness.

Existential Aloneness

Existential aloneness is an inherent aspect of being human. Many seek joy in external connections to avoid solitude, even though true happiness lies in embracing it. The reality is that no matter how many people surround you, a part of you will always be alone. Those who find peace in this aloneness radiate wholeness and elevate the lives of others. Life flows smoothly when fulfilment comes from within, rather than being sought externally. Fulfilment isn't about finding someone who completes you; it's about being so whole that others feel complete in your presence.

Life can be seen as a train journey, where companions come and go as the journey progresses.

Some leave at various "stations," bringing moments of joy or grief, while others join. Relationships shift, but the journey itself is continuous. From birth to death, you walk alone, even if you are surrounded by love. Accepting this inner solitude brings peace. It's in denying our existential aloneness that conflict arises; acceptance brings wholeness and harmony.

Embracing Existential Aloneness: A Three-Step Approach:

1. Accept Existential Aloneness

Many struggles stem from resisting inevitable truths: your aloneness, mortality, and the passage of time. By accepting these truths intellectually and emotionally, you reduce inner turmoil and experience deeper harmony. We should understand and accept that we came alone on this planet, a part of us is always alone, live alone, leave alone and come back alone - until perfection and purification of the vehicles of the body, mind and intellect.

2. Embrace Solitude Daily

Engage in daily activities that foster self-connection, as the Dalai Lama suggests: "spend time alone every day." Whether through peaceful walks, music, or simply sitting in nature, these moments cultivate inner contentment and a deeper connection with yourself.

3. Give Without Expectation

Start by nurturing one relationship selflessly, offering kindness without expecting emotional returns. This shifts relationships into spaces of genuine giving. Expanding this selflessness allows you to create a fulfilling world around you.

When you embrace existential aloneness, it becomes a source of immense strength. You become a beacon of light to others, like the sun, self-sufficient and whole. In solitude, you experience the universe's presence, realising that while you are alone, you are never truly isolated. Everything you need is within, waiting to be acknowledged and embraced.

CHAPTER 11
Sanatana Dharma: The Eternal Universal Principles

The term Dharma in Hinduism can be quite perplexing, as its meaning spans numerous pages in authentic Sanskrit dictionaries. Understanding Sanatana Dharma (the eternal order) and Svadharma (individual duty) offers clarity.

The Bhagavad Gita emphasises:

"Better one's own duty, even if imperfect, than the duty of another, even if well performed. Death in one's own duty is preferable; the duty of another brings fear and danger."

In the Einsteinian world of objects, everything has properties which can be classified as essential or non-essential. The essential property of a thing is what defines it—its very essence. Without it, the object ceases to be what it is. This defining essence is referred to as its Dharma.

For instance, the Dharma of sugar is its sweetness, and the Dharma of fire is its heat. Similarly, the Dharma of all living beings is the Self—the life force that makes one what they are. Without this life force, the body loses its vitality and becomes lifeless, soon disintegrating into nature. While alive, one may be physically active, mentally dynamic, and intellectually brilliant. But all these attributes depend on the presence of life, which is the supreme Dharma shared by all beings—plants, animals, and humans alike.

"This universal Dharma is referred to as Sanatana Dharma, the eternal and ancient principle from which all existence emerges." "It is the underlying reality, the divine essence that animates everything and resides within the heart of all beings."

Yet, despite sharing this universal essence, each individual is distinct. Why? Because every person carries their own unique tendencies (Vasanas) which shape their thoughts, actions, and character. These individual tendencies define one's Svadharma, or personal duty.

Sanatana Dharma represents the supreme universal truth—Brahman, the life force. On the other hand, Svadharma is the unique manifestation of one's personal Dharma, shaped by their innate tendencies. Your Svadharma determines whether your life exudes a fragrance of virtue or a stench of negativity, based on the qualities of your Vasanas.

Thus, the interplay between the universal Sanatana Dharma and individual Svadharma defines both our shared essence and personal journey. Reflect deeply—what is your Dharma, and how will you embody it?

Sanatana Dharma's timeless principles:

1. Eternal Truth: Beyond human concepts.

2. Unity: Interconnectedness of all.

3. Self-Realization: Inner reflection and growth.

4. Detachment: Letting go of attachments.

5. Present Moment: Embracing life's journey..

Sanatana Dharma guides seekers towards self-discovery, unity, and harmony with the universe.

CHAPTER 12
Spiritual Awakening: Experiencing Spiritual Transformation

Life transformation or spiritual awakening, renewal, metamorphosis, or radical change is a profound and enchanting process. Suddenly, you become aware of undergoing an internal awakening. Although the person remains unchanged physically, deep within spiritually, it feels akin to a butterfly emerging from its chrysalis. Transformation is a door that opens from within.

Spiritual awakening is a transformative process where one's perception shifts from separation to unity. It's a gentle unfolding of awareness, revealing the true nature of existence. As ego's veil lifts, the individual self merges with the universal consciousness. Inner peace, compassion, and wisdom flourish. The awakened heart recognises the divine in all, transcending boundaries and conditioning. With clarity and humility, one navigates life's challenges with grace. This profound shift frees us from suffering, igniting a deep sense of purpose and fulfilment. Spiritual awakening is a journey, not a destination – an eternal evolution of the soul.

CHAPTER 13
The Attitude of Gratitude: Cultivating Appreciation

There is a vast difference between need and want. Humans need food, clothing, shelter, and love—fundamental prerequisites for existence. These are basic needs. However, when these fundamentals are extended to, "I need a specific type of food from a specific place," or "I need a particular brand of clothing," or "I require an apartment of a certain size in a specific area," or "I need a car that must be a Suzuki, BMW, Mercedes, Audi, or Jaguar," the line between need and want becomes blurred. Similarly, while the need to be loved is fundamental, the desire to be loved by a specific person is a want. These specific preferences—"such and such"—represent wants, while the basics remain needs.

More than 70% of people in the world do not have even their fundamental needs met. Many of the remaining individuals have enough but still "want more." This desire for more is not inherently wrong. However, the core issue is the lack of an attitude of gratitude. People often fail to appreciate what they have, even when life has given them more than they ever expected. Instead of being thankful, they live in a state of dissatisfaction.

Some may think, "I'll only be happy if I own a Mercedes," or "I'll be happy only if I get an apartment in that particular area," or "I'll be happy only if I marry that specific person." They might say, "Only if I get that job, only if I get promoted, only if I receive a double raise, then I'll be happy." This endless cycle of "only if" thinking only leads to misery.

Happiness does not necessarily come from acquiring new external things. In reality, most people already have more than enough to sustain life. The dangerous thing we do is comparing with peers, neighbours, friends, and relatives who seem to have more than what we have. We don't know the insecurities they are facing!

What is needed is the ability to count one's blessings, to be content with what one already has, and to express gratitude to the Creator for life's design. Aspiring for more is natural, but it should be paired with being happy in the "here and now." A profound "thank you" now and then, to life and its Creator, fosters an attitude of gratitude, which, in turn, brings even more blessings than one could have ever dreamed of.

As the saying goes, the man who complained of having no shoes stopped his wailing when he saw someone without legs. In truth, many are fortunate. Embracing gratitude will bring not only enough but often much more than anticipated.

Thank you very much, in gratitude...

CHAPTER 14
Meditation: Cultivating Inner Peace

Meditation is a transformative practice cultivating inner peace, awareness, and balance. By training the mind, meditation helps connect with our inner self. Meditation is a tool to harmonise your mind, not control it. It's a journey of self-discovery and growth! Meditation is a process of taking you to the state which is "without a thought" so that it helps you dissolve in the Divine.

Meditation is a technique that:

1. Focuses on the present moment.

2. Quiets thoughts and emotions.

3. Cultivates awareness and clarity.

4. Develops inner peace and balance.

Illustrating the word Meditation through a metaphor: A Rose Garden

I am in the middle of a rose garden and it's all smelling of roses, and I am lost in the fragrance of the rose garden. I don't know something is happening to me just now, but it's happening. In the rose garden, the roses are transferring their fragrance to me, and I am not aware of it. I am so lost in the creation, so lost in the material reality, so lost in what I touch, smell; a celestial phenomenon is happening right now without my knowing about it. To know what happened to you when you were in the rose garden, you have to leave the rose garden.

Once you leave the rose garden and you wander away, you suddenly realise that you are smelling roses. You realise that the material reality is left behind but the spiritual essence of the rose has been smeared all over me and I came back smelling of roses. When I come back into the world after experiencing the meditative state, I will find myself a little more loving than I was ever before. I have more concentration, more clarity, more understanding, less anxiety; I know that the fragrance of the rose has poured onto me a little. You know that the fragrance of this rose is not mine; I did not have this before I went into the rose garden. I experience peace when I go into the State that I have not experienced before.

Earlier, we lived in this spiritual ignorance of everything of me and nothing of anything else. After this experience, you will find something of Him and something of me, and later on, you will realise there is no fragrance on my own. Everything of Him and nothing of me is Bliss, and that is Total Surrender.

In the **Rose Garden metaphor**, meditation is illustrated as the experience of being in the rose garden, surrounded by its beauty and fragrance. Meditation is:

1. Immersion in the present moment (lost in the fragrance).

2. Letting go of attachments and distractions (not aware of the fragrance transfer).

3. Connection with the divine or higher reality (Celestial phenomenon).

4. Transformation through inner peace and spiritual essence (fragrance of the rose).

5. Cultivation of love, concentration, clarity, and understanding.

The Meditator:

The meditator is the individual experiencing the rose garden. They are:

1. The seeker of spiritual growth and self-awareness.

2. Willing to let go of ego and attachments (lost in creation).

3. Open to transformation and inner peace.

4. Seeking connection with the divine.

5. Desiring total surrender and bliss.

Key Elements:

1. Rose Garden: Symbolises the meditative state

2. Fragrance: Represents inner peace, spiritual essence, and transformation.

3. Leaving the Garden: Integration of meditation's benefits into daily life.

4. Ishta Devata: Personal deity or higher power.

5. First-Fist: Direct experience of the divine or ultimate reality

Stages of Meditation:

1. Preparation (entering the garden).

2. Immersion (lost in fragrance).

3. Transformation (fragrance transfer).

4. Integration (Leaving the Garden).

5. Realisation (recognising the spiritual essence).

Benefits of Meditation.

1. Reduces stress and anxiety.

2. Improves mental clarity spind focus.

3. Enhances emotional well-being.

4. Boosts self-awareness and self-acceptance.

5. Supports physical health and well-being.

6. Increases productivity and creativity.

7. Fosters compassion and empathy.

8. Increased love and compassion.

9. Improved concentration and clarity.

Types of Meditation

1. Mindfulness Meditation (breath, body, or emotions)

2. Loving-Kindness Meditation (compassion and love)

3. Transcendental Meditation (mantras)

4. Guided Meditation (audio guidance)

5. Movement Meditation (yoga, tai chi, or walking).

6. Visualisation Meditation (imagining scenarios)

7. Chakra Meditation (energy centres)

Basic Meditation Technique

1. Find a quiet space.

2. Sit comfortably.

3. Close eyes.

4. Focus on breath

5. Acknowledge and release thoughts.

6. Continue for 5-30 minutes.

Step-by-Step Guide

Preparation

1. Set aside time and space.

2. Choose a technique

3. Sit comfortably.

Starting

1. Close your eyes.

2. Deep breaths.

3. Focus on breath.

During Meditation

1. Observe thoughts and emotions "without getting connected."

2. Release attachments

3. Refocus on breath.

Ending

1. Open eyes.

2. Deep breaths.

3. Notice feelings.

Tips for Beginners

1. Start short (5-10 minutes).

2. Be patient.

3. Make meditation a daily habit.

CHAPTER 15
Nature of the Spirit: Understanding Spiritual Essence

Everything begins with the Spirit. It can be compared to the eye of the storm, dynamic and always moving. The Spirit, or Atman, is the essence of our being, beyond body and mind. It's the spark of divine consciousness, connecting us to the universe. Timeless, spaceless, and eternal, the Spirit transcends duality and mortality. It's the source of intuition, wisdom, and inner peace. Unconditional love, compassion, and joy radiate from this core. The Spirit's presence is felt in moments of silence, awe, and connection. It guides us toward our true nature, urging us to let go of ego and limitations. Embracing the Spirit, we find freedom, unity, and our highest potential.

The nature of the spirit in Sanskrit is called Sat, Chit, Ananda, which is Existence, Consciousness, Bliss. Other names given are Transcendental Reality, God, Love, Consciousness, Enlivening Force, Tao, Chi, Qi, The Essence, Spiritual energy.

We are a bundle of joy and happiness. We all have a Spirit, and that Spirit makes life in us possible. We are all part of God. We are all Gods in disguise. Without God, we cannot, and without us, God will not. There is a big scheme in the universe, and the scheme is called evolution. There is a big scheme for a human being, and that is transformation. Transformation is a door that opens from inside. God is a part of the intricate design and is embedded in the design. We are all sparks of the same fire. (J. Krishnamurthi) Even if He wants to, He can't change the nature of the design now.

For example, Water boils at 100 degrees Centigrade. That which goes up has to come down because of gravity. There is no action rewind in life; life works on cause and effect. We are the creators of our own emotions; we are masters of creating our own free will. That which is born has to die and so on... Having designed the laws, He Himself has made Himself as part of the design as we all are. It is in our capacity to understand and align to such inexplicable laws to live a holistic life of being healthy, wealthy, wise, blissful, and enlightened. The only difference is our bodies die and so are mortal. Our spirit never dies and so-called immortal. When we greet and say "Namaste," bringing our two hands together, it means that the spirit in me and the spirit in you are one and the same.

There was no time in the past when I (God) or you or these rulers of men did not exist. Nor shall we ever cease to be hereafter. The essence in us, the touch of life in us never goes. It is permanent, eternal, immutable; it is God, the Highest Reality, in which each one of us has taken different forms. Just as the waves come and die away, but the ocean remains, our bodies would wither away because of ageing of our equipment – The body, the emotions, and our thoughts.

The body dies, but the impressions (Vasanas) in our subconscious mind after death will rest for some time until it finds a suitable place to burn and enter a suitable body to burn the Vasanas, and until all the Vasanas are burnt/exhausted, we will acquire new bodies. There are two important aspects in Hindu philosophy – Karma (Cause and Consequence) and Reincarnation (one soul, many bodies). The goal is to achieve Liberation, which means Nirvana, escape from bondage – cycles of birth and death.

CHAPTER 16
The Significance of Gayatri Mantra

The Gayatri Mantra is a powerful, transformative prayer that has shaped people's lives for centuries. This is the story of a warrior who became a yogi, of what unfolds when human power meets divine power, and ultimately, the story of a mantra. A mantra is more than just sound; it resonates through the body and mind, creating harmony that allows one to glimpse beyond the veil of maya, the illusion that conceals the Creator from creation. Mantras are believed to heal and elevate the spirit.

There are various mantras with different effects. A simple one is "Rama, Rama"; repeat it, and it brings an uplifted state. "Om Namah Shivaya," a six-syllable mantra, is said to destroy negative habits and grant strength. "Om Namo Bhagavate Vasudevaya," with twelve syllables, is designed to guide one inward, directing energy up the spine toward divine connection. The 32-syllable Mahamrityunjaya Mantra is considered a mantra of liberation. But among these, the Gayatri Mantra stands as an exalted, powerful, and benevolent mantra, filling devotees with grace and guiding them swiftly toward enlightenment.

The Gayatri Mantra, composed of 24 syllables, has been chanted for millennia by millions. When a Self-realised master communes with God with pure intention, God manifests in specific sounds. These sacred sounds are discovered in deep meditation. This is the story of the Gayatri Mantra: to whom it was given, and why.

In a distant era, the Satya Yuga, righteousness (Dharma) was strong and the voice of God was heard with ease. During this time, a king named Vishwamitra ruled. His name, meaning "friend of the universe," reflected his noble spirit. Under his leadership, his subjects prospered, lived in harmony, and maintained a close connection with nature. He was a just ruler, wielding power with fairness and compassion, and his undefeated army had expanded his domain significantly.

In those days, kings didn't stay confined to their palaces. They visited their territories to ensure prosperity and gain firsthand insights into their people's lives. After a nearly year-long tour, Vishwamitra's journey was ending, and he was pleased with his people's happiness. Before returning, he had one last visit to make, to a sage named Vasishta, who resided in a forest hermitage.

Vasishta was a Brahma Rishi—a title given to one with the highest spiritual realisation. In that era, kings looked after material well-being, while sages were responsible for spiritual guidance. Vasishta, Vishwamitra's spiritual adviser, lived in constant communion with God, and when he spoke, it was as if God's will was voiced through him.

As Vishwamitra entered the hermitage, he greeted Vasishta, who asked about the welfare of the kingdom. After an exchange of blessings, Vasishta offered Vishwamitra and his soldiers a banquet. Amused, the king accepted, though he saw no signs of provisions in the simple hermitage. Vasishta then addressed a sacred cow, which, at his word, miraculously produced a lavish feast.

After dining, Vishwamitra, astonished by the cow's power, asked Vasishta to give it to him, proposing to exchange a thousand cows and other riches. Vasishta refused, explaining that the cow was a divine gift meant to serve the needs of the hermitage, not for barter. Insistent, Vishwamitra grew angry and commanded his soldiers to seize the cow. But with Vasishta's blessing, the cow produced a celestial army that easily overpowered Vishwamitra's forces.

Humbled, Vishwamitra realised the limits of human power against divine might. Feeling defeated, he retreated to meditate on Lord Shiva, determined to acquire powers to surpass Vasishta. After hundreds of years of intense penance, Shiva granted him mastery over all elemental and celestial forces. Empowered, he returned to Vasishta's hermitage, unleashing fire, floods, and storms upon it, all of which Vasishta's staff absorbed.

In desperation, Vishwamitra released the Brahmastra, the most powerful cosmic weapon. Yet even this was absorbed by Vasishta's staff, a symbol of divine protection. Realising the futility of human power against true spiritual mastery, Vishwamitra's anger gave way to humility. He resolved to atone for his pride and sought a path to spiritual enlightenment.

With this new intention, Vishwamitra returned to the mountains, meditating for centuries, purging his heart of anger and desire. Eventually, Brahma appeared and granted him the title of "Rajarishi"—a king among sages. Disappointed that he had not achieved the title of Brahma Rishi, Vishwamitra continued his meditation, seeking answers within.

As his journey of self-inquiry continued, he uncovered the root of his anger: **attachment and desire.** Through deep self-reflection, he understood that attachment arose from dwelling on worldly things. To reach God, he had to dwell only on the Creator, not creation.

With renewed determination, Vishwamitra resumed his meditation, this time asking for divine guidance to serve humanity. His austerities reached such heights that finally, Lord Vishnu appeared, blessing him with the title of Brahma Rishi and giving him a simple wooden staff as a sign of divine communion.

Yet, Vishwamitra still sought a way to help humanity overcome suffering. Returning to meditation, he entered an ecstatic state, hearing a faint sound that grew into distinct syllables. This sound, the Gayatri Mantra, revealed itself as the remedy for human suffering—a powerful prayer that could part the veil of maya and reveal divine light.

With joy, Vishwamitra shared this mantra, knowing it would help countless people transcend sorrow and glimpse the Creator's bliss. Vasishta, who appeared in blessing, acknowledged Vishwamitra's role in bringing this divine gift to humanity. Thus, through Vishwamitra, the Gayatri Mantra was given to humanity as a pathway to enlightenment, its grace capable of revealing the eternal essence of the Creator.

The Gayatri Mantra:

ॐ

OM

(Sacred Syllable)

भूर्भुवःस्वः

BHUR BHUVAH SUVAHA

The material world, the physical world, the celestial world.

तत् सवितुर् वरेण्यं

TAT SAVITUR VARENIYAM

The Supreme Being is the source to be worshipped.

भर्गो देवस्य धीमहि

BHARGO DEVASYA DHEEMAHI

The Divine Light, its sacred truth, we deeply meditate.

धियो यो नःप्रचोदयात् ॥

DHIYO YO NAH PRACHODAYATH

The Intellect, which to us may Light be endowed.

CHAPTER 17
YOGA: Uniting Body, Mind and Spirit

The word Yoga means Union. Union in the spiritual context means union with God. The goal of a spiritual aspirant is Liberation or Samadhi, attaining the Supreme; it means getting out of the cycle of birth and death. This is the ultimate.

The four Yogas are ancient Indian spiritual paths that guide seekers towards union with the Divine. Each Yoga addresses a different aspect of human nature, providing a comprehensive approach to spiritual growth.

1. Bhakti Yoga (Devotional Yoga)

Focus: Heart and emotions.

Path: Love, devotion, and surrender to the Divine.

Practices: Chanting, singing, prayer, worship, and self-surrender.

Goal: Cultivate love and devotion, transcending ego and attachment.

The Devoted Musician:

A poor musician, Ram, lived in a temple town. His sole passion was playing the veena (stringed instrument) to worship Lord Krishna.

Ram's devotion was unwavering;

1. Selfless Love: He played for Krishna, not for fame or wealth.

2. Unwavering Dedication: Daily, he'd play with intense passion.

3. Surrender: He offered his music as a humble offering.

One evening, Krishna appeared disguised as a traveller.

"Ram, your music has captivated me," Krishna said. "Request anything,"

Ram replied, "Lord, I seek nothing. Playing for you is my joy."

Krishna smiled, "Your Bhakti (devotion) has freed you. You've realised true union."

2. Karma Yoga (Action Yoga)

Focus: Mind and actions.

Path: Selfless service, detachment, and equanimity.

Practices: Selfless work, volunteerism, and mindfulness in daily activities.

Goal: Develop detachment, balance, and inner peace through selfless action.

The Selfless Sweeper:

A humble sweeper, Lakshman, worked tirelessly at a temple. His duties included cleaning, gardening, and serving pilgrims.

One day, a wise sage asked Lakshman, "Do you seek enlightenment?"

Lakshman replied, "I simply serve, without expectation."

The sage smiled, "Your selfless actions are Karma Yoga. You've transcended attachment to outcomes."

The key principles of Karma Yoga—selfless action, detachment, dedication, and equanimity— are more relevant today than ever, especially as we often find ourselves stressed by not fully understanding the workings of the universe. It's important to recognise that while we have control over our actions, the outcomes are beyond our control. Life follows the law of cause and effect, or choice and consequence: while we can choose our actions, the consequences unfold independently. These consequences fall into four possible categories:

1. Greater than what we desired.

2. Exactly what we desired.

3. Less than what we desired.

4. The opposite of what we desired.

With each consequence, we gain insight and can make new choices, setting off new possibilities and awaiting fresh outcomes. Embracing our free will to choose from endless possibilities while surrendering to the wisdom embedded in each outcome reflects "Intelligent Living." This is the harmony of choice and surrender, balancing our efforts with trust in the infinite wisdom of a higher will.

3. Raja Yoga (Royal Yoga)

Focus: Mind and Meditation

Path: Mind control, concentration, and inner awareness.

Practices: Meditation, pranayama, and introspection.

Goal: Achieve mental clarity, inner peace, and self-realisation

An enlightening story illustrating Raja Yoga:

The Eight-fold Path

A seeker, Raj, sought enlightenment from sage Raghavan.

Raghavan taught Raj the eight limbs of Raja Yoga:

1. Yamas: (Ethical living - non-violence, truthfulness, non-stealing, continence, non-coveting).

2. Niyamas: (Personal disciplines - Purity, contentment, self-discipline, self-reflection, self-surrender).

3. Asanas: Physical postures.

4. Pranayama: Breath control.

5. Pratyahara: Sense withdrawal.

6. Dharana: Concentration.

7. Dhyana: Meditation.

8. Samadhi: Union with the divine.

Raj diligently practiced transcending:

1. Ego.

2. Attachments.

3. Dualities.

Raghavan smiled, "Raj, you've realised Raja Yoga's essence: union with the Self."

4. Jnana Yoga (Knowledge Yoga)

Focus: Intellect and wisdom.

Path: Inquiry, reflection, and discernment.

Practices: Study of scriptures, self-inquiry, and contemplation.

Goal: Attain wisdom, discern reality, and transcend ignorance.

Here's an enlightening story illustrating Gnana Yoga:

The Discerning Seeker

A seeker, Vasu, sought wisdom from sage Vidya.

Vasu asked, "What is the ultimate reality?"

Vidya replied, "Seek within. Discriminate between permanent and impermanent, real and unreal."

Vasu contemplated, distinguishing:

1.   Permanent (Brahman): Unchanging essence.

2.   Impermanent (Maya): Ever-changing world.

3.   Real (Sat): Eternal truth.

4.   Unreal (Asat): Illusory appearances.

Vidya smiled, "Vasu, your discernment (Viveka) illuminates Gnana Yoga's path." Gnana Yoga helps self-inquiry, discrimination (Viveka), detachment (Vairagya), and mental clarity (Manonasa).

How the four Yogas help reach God:

1. Integration: The 4 Yogas integrate physical, emotional, mental, and intellectual aspects, preparing the seeker for union with the Divine.

2. Purification: Each yoga helps purify the body, heart, mind, and intellect, removing obstacles to spiritual growth.

3. Self-Realization: Through these Yogas, seekers realise their true nature, transcending ego and limitations.

4. Devotion and Love: Bhakti Yoga cultivates love and devotion, essential for union with the Divine.

5. Inner Transformation: The 4 Yogas facilitate inner transformation, enabling seekers to embody divine qualities.

6. Direct Experience: These Yogas provide direct experience of the Divine beyond intellectual understanding.

CHAPTER 18
Who is God: Exploring the Concept of God

All Religions say that God is not a person but a Formless Presence. If there is a creation, there has to be a Creator; we may call it God, Spirit, Transcendental Reality, Consciousness, The Enlivening Force, The Spiritual Energy, The Essence and so on. God or anything we call that energy is Formless. Formless gives rise to form. For every life present anywhere on our planet, there has to be a "Formless" component to keep it alive. In the presence of the Formless, all Forms function.

We will take science to establish this truth:

If I want to know about King Alexander, we have to go back in history to the time during which Alexander lived, and then I will understand Alexander.

If I want to know about King Ashoka, I have to study the history of the time during which King Ashoka lived.

If you want to study God, you have to study the time in which God was there – then you will know God.

Somehow God should have been there, so let's go to the beginning. It is not in 2024; God should have been there much before that! So, could it be the first year.

To study Time we need to define Time. Albert Einstein said, "Time is the interval between two events." Rishis said that Time is the interval between two events during my time. Events that are happening in my life are experiences. So, Time is the interval between two experiences. An experience is not an experience if it does not trigger a Thought. So, Time is the interval between two Thoughts. On the second Thought, there is Time, whereas in the first Thought, there is no Time. (Zero) To take a metaphor: The distance between Chennai and Mumbai is 1200. Distance at Mumbai is 1200 Kms. Distance at Chennai is Zero since it is the origin.

So, could God have been there in the first year? No, it's not possible because in the first year there are 365 days. So, God could have been on the first day? No, since on the first day there are 24 hours. So, God could have been in the first hour. But God could not have been there because in the first hour there are 60 minutes, so, God should have been in the first minute since in the first minute there are

60 seconds. So, God should have been there in the first second. How is it possible!?...

That First-First is God. If there is creation, there has to be a Creator. Effect is nothing but Cause in a different form, a different manifestation. The Creator is embedded in a different form in the creation. God created the human being in his own image; it means that in every Jivatma (individual soul) some Paramatma (oversoul) is deposited. *"Aham Brahmasmi or I am God"* is the culture of this land (Bharat) which says that everything is to be worshipped. So, Worship Thyself. Worship the Moon, the Sun, parents, children, spouse, relatives, friends, stone, buffalo, Cow, Lion, elephant and everything... In Hinduism, there are more Gods than people!! We are all sparks of the same fire, said J. Krishnamoorthy, one of the greatest philosophers. In every form, the Formless is present. Only in the presence of the Formless, the Form functions; otherwise not.

The First-First is God. The First Second is Thought. The unit of time is that's perhaps why called second!! On the First-First, there is no time, no space but only God. So, how to reach the First-First? It is through Yoga. Yoga in this context means union with God. Some of the Yogas are Gnana Yoga, Bhakti Yoga, Raja Yoga, Karma Yoga, Mantra yoga and Tantra Yoga. The eight-fold path of Patanjali, also known as Ashtanga yoga, is the best way to reach the First-First (Samadhi). Meditation is a process of taking you to the First-First, which is without a Thought, so that helps you dissolve into the *Divine*.

The First-First is Truth

The First-First is Love.

The First-First is beyond Time, beyond Distance.

God is a reality beyond Time and Space.

Since we as humans cannot conceptualise the wholeness and Oneness of the Infinite Formless, to objectify our limited capacity to comprehend the Whole, we have objects and worship. Faith plays a very important role in understanding the existence of God.

Who is God to you?

The Search for God:

A seeker, eager to understand God, approached a wise sage.

"Who is God?" the seeker asked.

The sage smiled, "Go to the village and ask anyone you meet, 'Who is God?' Then return."

The seeker did so.

A priest replied, "God is the divine creator."

A philosopher said, "God is the universe's essence."

A villager said, "God is love."

The seeker returned to the sage, confused.

The sage smiled, "Now, go to the river and ask the water, 'Who is God?'"

The seeker did. The river's gentle flow seemed to whisper, "I am God's reflection."

Returning, the seeker asked, "What does this mean?"

The sage explained:

"God is beyond human comprehension. God transcends definitions. God is in everything."

God is:

1.   The universe's essence: In every atom.

2.   Love: Binding humanity.

3.   Creator: Crafting existence.

4.   Reflection: In nature's beauty.

God is beyond words, yet reflected in all."

The seeker's eyes widened, understanding.

God's essence transcends human understanding. Yet, God's presence permeates everything. He is both with Form although remaining Formless. Faith is the bridge connecting our limited self (ego) with the Formless God.

CHAPTER 19
Man is not Different from God: Realising Unity with the Divine

The profound statements of the Vedas, such as:

- Aham Brahmasmi (I am Brahman)

- Prajnanam Brahma (Brahman is Supreme Consciousness)

- Tat Twam Asi (That Thou Art)

- Ayam Atma Brahma (This Self is Brahman)

Guide us toward the path of unity, oneness, and divinity. Let's delve deeper.

If there is creation, there has to be a Creator. If there is an effect, there has to be a cause. Effect is nothing but Cause in a different form, a different manifestation. The Creator is embedded in a different form in the creation. God created the human being in his own image, it means that in every Jivatma (individual soul) some Paramatma (universal soul) is deposited. 'Aham Brahmasmi,' I am God is the culture of this land which says that everything is to be worshipped. So, Worship Thyself. Worship the Moon, the Sun, parents, children, spouse, relatives, friends, stone, buffalo, cow, lion, elephant and everything... In Hinduism there are more Gods than people!! J. Krishnamurti, one of the greatest philosophers, said that we are all sparks of the same fire.

Here's a modern story that illustrates the concept of being a part of God:

The Smartphone and the Network:

A young woman named Sanvi was scrolling through social media on her smartphone. She felt restless and disconnected, even though she was surrounded by friends and family. Life felt hectic, and in her rush to keep up, she felt more alone than ever, like a tiny, isolated part of the world that didn't really matter.

One evening, Sanvi had a strange dream. She saw herself as her smartphone, trying desperately to connect to Wi-Fi but failing. She felt stuck, cut off from everything. She started to panic.

Then, a voice spoke to her gently, saying, "You don't need to try so hard. Just look within. The connection is already there."

Puzzled, Sanvi looked closer and realised that her smartphone was part of a massive network, like an ocean of data connecting everyone, everywhere.

She didn't have to search for it; she just had to turn on her "connection."

The voice continued, "You are a part of this network, and every message, call, and piece of information flows through it. You're connected with everyone and everything. You may seem like a single device, but you are a part of a vast, invisible whole."

Sanvi woke up with a new perspective. She realised that, like her phone is connected to an invisible network, she, too, was connected to something greater—a divine source, the essence of life, or God. All the people, places, and things around her were part of that same "network," and even though she felt like just one individual, she was a piece of something infinite, meaningful, and interconnected.

In our modern, digital world, we're often focused on devices, connections, and networks. But this story reminds us that just as every device connects to a vast network, each of us is connected to the divine—a part of God, bound together with others in a greater, unbreakable whole.

CHAPTER 20

Navigating Certainty and Uncertainty: Embracing Change

Life is a dynamic interplay between certainty and uncertainty. While certainty offers a comforting sense of stability, uncertainty provides the excitement of possibility and the opportunity for growth. Understanding how to balance these forces is essential for a meaningful life.

Certainty has always been a fundamental human need. From ancient times, we have sought to predict and control our environment to feel safe. We make plans, set goals, and establish routines because they give us a sense of control. In business and leadership, certainty builds trust and ensures smoother operations. When leaders provide clarity, teams know what to expect and how to act. On a personal level, we all need some degree of certainty: knowing we have a roof over our heads, food on the table, and a predictable routine to follow. These basics allow us to function and build a sense of self-assurance.

However, life is rarely entirely predictable. Unexpected events like a sudden job loss, a global pandemic, or a change in relationships can shift our sense of certainty. Here is where uncertainty comes into play. It can feel unsettling, even frightening. The human mind often dislikes ambiguity, and the lack of clarity can give rise to anxiety and stress. Yet, uncertainty is also the birthplace of creativity, innovation, and transformation. Without it, life would be stagnant, devoid of surprises, and lacking growth.

Belief in a higher power, often understood as spirituality or God, offers a profound sense of solace by helping us see life's intricate design through deeper connections—a connection with the Divine or Higher Self.

The concept of spirituality and God plays a profound role in helping us navigate the realms of certainty and uncertainty. Here's how:

Spirituality and Certainty

Spirituality provides a sense of certainty that goes beyond the material or logical aspects of life. For many, the belief in a higher power or universal intelligence offers comfort and stability. Spiritual practices, such as meditation, prayer, or rituals, create a structured routine that reinforces this sense of order and assurance. The teachings of various spiritual traditions often emphasise that there is a divine plan or purpose, which can be a source of strength and certainty when facing life's challenges. This idea reassures us that even when we don't understand everything, there is a higher wisdom at work.

For example, many religious and spiritual philosophies teach that certain values—like love, compassion, truth, and integrity—are unwavering and eternal. These provide a moral compass and a stable foundation that helps individuals make decisions and maintain their purpose even in unpredictable situations.

Spirituality and Uncertainty

On the flip side, spirituality also encourages us to embrace and find meaning in uncertainty. Many spiritual traditions acknowledge that life is inherently unpredictable and that suffering often arises from the illusion of complete control. The Bhagavad Gita, for instance, teaches us to perform our duties without attachment to the results, accepting that some outcomes are beyond our influence. This practice helps us release anxiety and trust in the unfolding of life.

God or the concept of a higher power often serves as a reminder of the mystery and the beauty of the unknown. In moments of uncertainty, faith can offer solace. Trusting that there is a divine will or a greater purpose behind our experiences invites us to surrender, be present, and grow spiritually. Embracing uncertainty thus becomes a spiritual exercise in humility, patience, and hope.

Balance Through Spiritual Grounding

Spirituality can act as a bridge between certainty and uncertainty. It offers rituals, values, and teachings that ground us, yet it also encourages us to step into the unknown with courage and curiosity. A spiritual or philosophical foundation provides inner strength to adapt and thrive when life feels chaotic. It invites us to anchor our sense of identity and purpose in something greater than our immediate circumstances, empowering us to navigate life's highs and lows with grace.

In summary, spirituality and the concept of God offer both the security of knowing there is a guiding force in the universe and the wisdom to appreciate the unknown. It's a harmonious dance, where the faithful learn to be rooted yet flexible, assured yet open, and confident yet humble. This balance ultimately enriches our human experience and enables us to live fully.

Here's a thought-provoking story:

The River's Wisdom

A seeker, Ravi, asked a wise sage, "How can I find certainty in life's uncertainties?"

The sage took Ravi to a river.

"Observe," the sage said. "The river's surface changes constantly, yet its depths remain calm."

Ravi realised:

1. Uncertainty: Life's surface is unpredictable (waves, currents).

2. Certainty: Inner truth and essence remain steady (river's depths).

The sage smiled, "Embrace uncertainty, anchor in self-awareness."

CHAPTER 21

Our Conscience: Listening to Inner Guidance

Human beings and animals differ in many ways, yet they share certain fundamental similarities. Both have sensory faculties—eyes, ears, skin, nose, and tongue—through which they see, hear, feel, smell, and taste the world around them. Life's evolutionary journey has progressed from the mineral realm to plants, then to animals, and ultimately to humans.

What sets humans apart from animals is their unique faculty, the "Intellect," which enables them to discern right from wrong. Humans are expected to uphold morals, ethics, and values—concepts that animals lack. Morals and values are typically personal, while ethics often apply in professional or societal contexts.

One essential human quality is "Conscience," the mental faculty that discerns between right and wrong. More than just an instinct, conscience acts as a moral compass. A story illustrates this:

A seasoned thief, who lived with his wife and son, aspired for his son to follow in his footsteps.

Not merely a thief, he wanted his son to become a "master thief," establishing a legacy of skill. After years of training his son in the subtle art of thievery, he felt it was time for a final test. He gave his son an address and instructed him to break in, steal valuables, and return undetected.

Anxious yet determined, the son left at 11 p.m., executed the theft skillfully, and began his journey back. But as he walked away, a strange feeling overtook him – he felt as though everything around him was watching. He realised it wasn't just the moon or the trees, but his own conscience observing him.

At dawn, he returned home empty-handed, to his father's dismay. He explained, "As I walked away with the valuables, my conscience watched me. I couldn't go on." He confessed his discomfort with the life of theft and expressed a desire to pursue a more honest path, leaving his father bewildered yet introspective.

This story reminds us that, though our actions may seem hidden, our conscience, the "Silent Witness," sees all. Our soul is connected to the entire universe, and every action resonates beyond ourselves. This is how the law of karma—the law of cause and effect—unfolds: as we sow, so shall we reap.

Conscience, often regarded as the voice of the divine within, guides us. As Lao Tzu reminds us:

"Watch your thoughts; they become words."

Watch your words; they become actions.

Watch your actions; they become habits.

Watch your habits; they become your character.

Watch your character; it becomes your destiny."

And as Einstein wisely observed, "Never do anything against conscience, even if the state demands it." Let us act nobly, for our actions shape our destiny.

CHAPTER 22
Spirituality: Introducing Spiritual Principles

This chapter talks about Oneness. "We are all One; we are all sparks of the same fire." - J. Krishnamurti. This alone is Spirituality.

The quality of being concerned with the human spirit or soul as opposed to material or physical things is spirituality. Spirituality is a personal journey to discover meaning and purpose in life. It involves aligning ourselves with the fundamental principles of life.

Everything that has life starts with the spirit, which is the vital force that makes our existence possible. Spirituality is about feeling connected to something greater than ourselves. This can include practices like increasing self-awareness, finding inner peace, exploring nature, and pondering important questions like the purpose of life and why we are here.

Ultimately, the goal is to gain a deeper understanding of life, the universe, and our place in it. Oneness is the same meaning of Spirituality. Nothing can be more to the point than Annie Besant's Universal prayer of The Theosophical Society in 1923, and it reads as:

'O Hidden Life vibrant in all atoms

'O Hidden Light shining in every creature

'O Hidden Love embracing all in Oneness

May each who feels himself as one with Thee.

Knows that he is also one with everyone else.

Reflect on these two stories:

Story 1: The River of Life

Once, in a small village nestled between two great mountains, there lived a young seeker named Vivek. Vivek felt an insatiable hunger to understand the mysteries of life and the universe.

One day, while wandering through the forest, Vivek stumbled upon a wise old sage named Dharmesh. Dharmesh's eyes sparkled with an otherworldly energy, and his presence radiated peace.

"Sage Dharmesh, I seek answers," Vivek said. "What is the essence of life?"

Dharmesh smiled. "Life is like a river, Vivek. It flows, ever-changing, yet remaining constant. Its source is the divine, and its destination is the same."

Vivek pondered this. "What about spirituality? How do we connect with the divine?"

"Spirituality is the current that runs through the river," Dharmesh replied. "It's the energy that guides us, nourishes us, and transforms us. We connect through intention, compassion, and mindfulness."

Vivek's curiosity deepened. "And what about energy? Is it the same as spirit?"

"Energy is the vibration that underlies all existence," Dharmesh explained. "It's the thread that weaves together every particle, every thought, and every emotion. Spirit is the essence that animates energy, giving it purpose and direction."

As they walked along the riverbank, Dharmesh pointed to a rapid. "See how the water churns and foams? That's like the turmoil of our minds. But observe the calm depths beneath. That's the serenity of our true nature."

Vivek felt a profound shift within. "I understand. Life is a dance between energy and spirit."

Dharmesh nodded. "And you, Vivek, are the dancer. Your every step, every breath, and every thought influence the river's flow."

From that day forward, Vivek lived with a newfound sense of purpose and harmony. He flowed with the river, attuned to its rhythms, and radiated the energy of its true spirit.

Story 2: The Luminous Thread

In a small village nestled between two great mountains, there lived a young woman named Anusha. She felt an innate connection to the natural world and sensed that life was more than what met the eye.

One day, while wandering through the forest, Anusha stumbled upon a wise old sage named Vedika. His eyes sparkled with an otherworldly energy, and his presence radiated peace.

"Sage Vedika, Anusha, I seek answers," Anusha said. "What is the essence of life?"

"Life is a thread of energy," Vedika replied. "It weaves together every moment, every thought, and every emotion. This thread is luminous, and its radiance nourishes the world."

Anusha pondered this. "How do we connect with this thread?"

"Through intention, compassion, and mindfulness," Vedika said, "as you cultivate these qualities, your energy resonates with the thread, illuminating your path."

Anusha's curiosity deepened. "What about spirituality? How do we nurture it?"

"Spirituality is the harmony between your energy and the universe," Vedika explained. "It's the symphony of vibrations, where every note resonates with the divine."

As they walked, Vedika pointed to a river. "See how the water flows, effortlessly connecting with every rock, every bend? That's the flow of life, Anusha. Spirituality is surrendering to this flow."

Anusha felt a profound shift within. "I understand. Life is a dance of energy, and spirituality is the rhythm."

Vedika smiled. "And you, Anusha, are the dancer. Your every step, every breath, and every thought influence the thread's luminosity."

From that day forward, Anusha lived with a newfound sense of purpose and harmony. She wove her energy with the thread, radiating light and nourishing the world.

Here's a poignant story illustrating spiritual growth:

Story 3: The Lotus Flower

A young monk, frustrated with his spiritual progress, approached his master.

"Master, I've meditated for years, yet I feel no closer to enlightenment," he said.

The master smiled, "Visit the lotus pond. Observe the flower's journey."

The monk did. He noticed:

1. Roots in mud: The lotus grew from murky depths.

2. Stem through water: It rose through the pond's challenges.

3. Blooming above: The flower blossomed, radiant, above the water.

The master explained:

"Your spiritual journey mirrors the lotus:

1. Roots: Your experiences shape you.

2. Stem: You navigate life's challenges.

3. Bloom: Self-realization, inner peace, and spiritual awakening emerge."

The monk realised:

Spirituality isn't escaping life, but:

1. Embracing experiences.

2. Learning from challenges.

3. Cultivating inner peace.

Summarising, the key takeaways from the three stories:

1. Life is an interconnected web of energy.

2. Spirituality is harmony with the universe. It is also the guiding force that connects us to the divine.

3. Energy is the vibration that underlies all of existence.

4. Our thoughts and emotions influence the world.

5. Intention, compassion, and mindfulness cultivate the connection.

6. Every moment is an opportunity for connection.

CHAPTER 23
The Prayer

A prayer is a heartfelt communication with a higher power, divine being, or the universe, expressing: Gratitude; Requests; Confessions; Praise; Intentions. Prayers can connect us with the divine, promoting a sense of unity and oneness. Provide solace and emotional healing. Foster gratitude, humility, and self-awareness. Guide decision-making and intuition.

The king and his top ministers once ventured deep into the forest for a hunting expedition. After a successful hunt, they rested under the shade of a towering tree, enjoying their lunch and the calm, unaware that a hungry lion lurked nearby. Suddenly, a thunderous roar shattered the peace, sending the king and his ministers scrambling in fear. They sprinted as fast as they could, but the lion was faster and quickly closed in on them. Within striking distance of just 36 feet, the lion prepared to pounce on the king, who lagged slightly behind. Sensing his fate, the king closed his eyes, said a final prayer, and braced for the end.

Just then, a rustling sound and a pained roar from the lion broke the silence. The king opened his eyes to a surprising sight—a hunter who had been passing through the forest saw the king's predicament and, with swift precision, released a poisoned arrow. It struck the lion, bringing it down instantly. Overwhelmed with gratitude, the king embraced the hunter and offered him gold, gems, silver, land—whatever he desired. But the hunter, calm and humble, simply said, "Thank you, Your Majesty, but I ask only one thing: please visit my home one day."

The king was touched by the simplicity of the request, considering the life-saving service he had just received. Reflecting on his upcoming birthday, he promised the hunter he would celebrate it at his home, and, with a final embrace, returned to the palace with his ministers.

The next day, the ministers, eager to prepare for the king's visit, inspected the hunter's humble dwelling in the forest. To their surprise, it was a modest bamboo hut with thatched roofing, a temporary shelter at best. Deciding this was no place for a royal visit, they set about constructing a grand house—one with high ceilings, large doors and windows, fine furniture, and silverware. They even adorned the space with precious stones to convey opulence befitting the king's arrival.

When the king arrived at the hunter's home on his birthday, he was accompanied by his entire court. The king expressed his gratitude, showering the hunter with gifts of gold, gemstones, a large forest estate, and weaponry for his protection. He also gifted the hunter fine horses and invited him to visit the palace someday.

Though deeply grateful, the hunter had only ever desired the king's presence in his humble home, not wealth or treasures. Yet he received far more than he could have imagined, forging a lasting bond with the king.

This story holds a lesson for us all. Instead of asking God for specific things, we think we need, we can offer sincere thanks for what He's already given and invite Him into our hearts with humility and gratitude. In doing so, we trust that He knows what we need far better than we do and will provide us with the strength and tools to live a fulfilled life.

The best prayer would be to thank God for all the blessings He has already bestowed upon us; follow up with "May all beings on the planet be happy." *Lokah samastah sukhino bhavantu* (Sanskrit: लोकः समस्ताः सुखिनो भवन्तु) is a Sanskrit mantra that is often chanted at the conclusion of a yoga practice. It means "may everyone in the whole world be happy."

As Mahatma Gandhi once said, "It is better in prayer to have a heart without words than words without a heart." True prayer is a lifting of the heart and mind to God, a deep yearning of the soul, not merely a list of desires.

CHAPTER 24
What is Spiritual Evolution: Increasing Energy Levels

Sometimes we see people succeeding in life. It appears that there is no logic to success. I have seen very capable people, highly educated people with a lot of advantages not succeeding. And also, we see people who can't talk properly and their extraordinary success startles you. It seems there is no logic. It seems that everything that is happening in life is random. However, there is an order to this randomness, there is an order to this chaos.

There is an existential hierarchy which supersedes all manmade hierarchies, and there is a spiritual dimension to energy. Material is form, spiritual is formless. Spiritual can neither be defined nor confined. There is a formless presence in all the functions in which everything functions, but how we make it function is spiritual evolution. Spiritual evolution is not wearing a colour of clothes, not because he knows a few slokas, not because he has been given a position in the temple, not because he is wearing some symbols of religion. Spiritual evolution is, even if you are a monkey, you should know how to make it work for you. Nothing can be closer to truth than this. Spiritual evolution is to delegate it to God and get it done. It is not God who makes this faith work, my faith that makes my God work for me, the extent to which I grow in my faith, my God has to work for me.

The laws of spiritual energy that govern our life are

1. The lower in energy would be drawn towards the higher in energy, and the higher in energy would always empower the lower in energy. When you align with this law, material evolution is not a problem at all.

2. When your energy level is increased, you will always be pushed higher and deeper. This is Spiritual evolution.

Without the second law, spiritual evolution is not possible even if you learn sastras, do a PhD in Jainology, or go to seminary schools and learn or do Namaz five times, fast, etc...

As you draw more ramergy, you will be drawing all the lower in energy. People come in search of you. Not in a political perspective, from a corporate set up itself, good people should come and work for you.

Opportunities come in search of you, Investments come in search of you. Your responsibility will be to grow higher in energy. I will start drawing the best in my life. That's why it is very confusing seeing the results various people produce. In the intangible existential hierarchy, all those who are lower in energy will be drawn by the higher in energy. Gandhi had a feminine voice; he was not a great communicator, yet he was a very powerful person.

Almost looks like the contract would come, but it doesn't. The person confided that he would join but did not join. Just increase the energy level. All the rivers will come to the ocean. A gesture is enough to empower people; everything at this materialistic level will change to your advantage.

When the energy level is increased, you are pushed higher and deeper - Consider a U tube. Water finds its own level. When you fill up water on one side, the other side also fills up to the same level. Make markings on one side indicating the level of water and on the other side indicate Physical, Mental, Intellectual, emotional, and Spiritual. As the water rises on one side, it increases on the other side also. When energy levels increase, correspondingly, our personalities get to change from Physical personality, Mental persmality, Intellectual personality, emotional personality, and spiritual personality.

Physical personality - Although you have a human form, you still operate by instincts and not by intelligence. Everything in life concerns your body only. Bed, food, weather, sex, flesh, lust; nothing is beyond the body, always craving to touch. Eating, sleeping, excreting, and sensuality are the only occupations. Very low energy levels. I am sure none of you will fall into this category.

Mental Personality - When the energy level increases, it becomes that stage of indulgence and repetitiveness of an experience. Many of you would be in this level. You will see the same movie seven times. You will go to the same restaurant always. You will eat the same menu all the time. You will go to the same holiday spot every year. You will have the same friends. You will have six coffees per day and so on. In this stage, the man is half man and half animal.

When the energy level increases, you get identified with the intellectual personality. Versatility, varied experiences, and this shift make it easy to choose between what is right and what is easy. Choosing right over wrong becomes very easy for you regardless of whether it is a pleasurable or a painful situation. You will have a new clarity with which you see things. For most of us, chaos is not because we don't have an answer but because we have so many answers. CONFUSION IS WEAKNESS;

CLARITY IS POWER. It is not difficult to take standpoints - knowing when to be a consequence receiver or when to be a choice maker. There is no ambiguity at all. The world will approach you for clarity. You will find it easy to come up with solutions. You have the power of choice - and become responsible for life.

From the intelligent personality to the emotional personality or feeling personality, you start feeling beautiful within. When your feelings are beautiful, your Being is beautiful. When your being is beautiful, you are beautiful. Love is no more a choice. A rose does not decide to give its fragrance; spreading its fragrance becomes its nature. The radiance of the sun is its nature. Love, peace, bliss, and forgiveness become your nature. Even if you want to be bad, you can't be bad. Love oozes from you. Whatever you see, you see through the spectacles of love. There is a state of Bliss. You are Ananda. It's not that you chose to be compassionate, compassion becomes your very nature. At that state when you were in the mental state you were half man, half animal, in the emotional state you become half man, and half Divine. One leg is still in the intellectual quality of life. You will feel Divinity in every aspect of life. In fact, you start romancing life. In every cell of your system, you can feel Life is Beautiful. For all this, do you have to master any scriptures? Nothing at all. It's just that your energy levels will have to be increased and when your energy is increased, you are automatically pushed higher and deeper.

When the energy level increases further at the spiritual level, the river has merged into the ocean and becomes the ocean. The duality is removed. Me and my father are one and the same as Christ used to say. There is no cosmic divide in this phenomenon anymore. Perennial flow happens. When you reach that stage, it is not the energy flow to you, you become the energy source for others. You are the ocean and all the rivers come into you. The river has merged into the ocean and has become the ocean. Sugar has gone into the coffee and has become the coffee. It is Divinity in human form.

CHAPTER 25
The Purpose of Life

The universe exists for evolution, and humanity's purpose is transformation. Life calls us to explore the "why" of our existence—why we are here on this planet and how we should use this incredible opportunity we've been given. A person's purpose can evolve over time, and each of us may find multiple purposes along the way. Ultimately, the journey is one of transformation, from "animal-man" to "true human," and finally, toward the divine and becoming divine.

In various contexts, Purpose Answers 'THE WHY':

1. Personal purpose: Why am I here? What drives me?

2. Project purpose: Why are we undertaking this initiative?

3. Product purpose: Why does this exist? What problem does it solve?

4. Existential purpose: Why do we exist? What's life's meaning?

Answering 'THE WHY' provides:

1. Direction.

2. Motivation

3. Focus.

4. Clarity

You should know where you are going is a famous adage. If you do not know where you are going, any road can take you there. "THE WHY answers the purpose: Why should I do this? A strong answer to the WHY gives a strong enough purpose."

Some stories to reflect upon:

1. A man was working as an electrician and was working for long hours. Someone asked him why he was working such long hours. The electrician answered, "I am working long hours so that I can earn more money and with money, I can give a better standard of life to my family and better education to my children." This electrician's purpose is to provide a good standard of life for his family and good education for his children.

2. Rajesh gave up his lucrative job in the US and came back to India to look after his aged parents. Looking after his parents was his purpose.

3. Virat completed his PhD in aeronautical engineering from one of the premier institutes and joined The Ashram. Doing a PhD was his parents' wish, but he was more interested in God Realisation. His purpose in life was God Realisation.

4. I quit my business in 2010 when I was 52 and joined the Theosophical Society and Ramakrishna Mutt to serve in honorary positions. My purpose was to do service without expectations.

Here's another thought-provoking story:

The Potter's Wheel

A young apprentice fascinated by pottery asked his master:

"Master, what's the purpose of life?"

The master smiled, "Watch closely."

He spun the potter's wheel, shaping clay into vessels.

"Some vessels hold water, others hold flowers, and some merely decorate," he said.

Their purposes differ, yet all:

1. Emerge from the same clay (shared humanity).

2. Requires shaping (growth, learning).

3. Serve unique functions (individual purposes).

4. Reflect the creator's craftsmanship (divine connection).

Your purpose unfolds similarly:

1. Discover your inherent strengths (clay).

2   Shape yourself through experiences (wheel).

3. Find your unique function (service).

4. Reflect the divine within (connection).

Life is a **"LILA"**, also known as a divine play in which all beings are actors upon a grand stage. Crafted in the image of the Creator, this world is both a mirror and a canvas—a place where humans are meant to rise above the animalistic instincts within them and embody the highest ideals of humanity. In doing so, they reflect the divine qualities of compassion, wisdom, and selflessness. An ideal human being, in this sense, is not merely one who lives well but one who mirrors the virtues of the Creator, embodying love, kindness, and strength.

Every person is born with a purpose: to realise their fullest potential in the external world while uniting with the infinite Consciousness within. This journey of self-actualisation requires cultivating the mind, mastering the emotions, and sharpening the intellect so that each thought and action moves closer to expressing divinity. As one grows inwardly, there is a natural expansion outward, and they become a positive force for others.

Throughout life, the highest goal should be to elevate oneself and serve others, embracing an inclusive compassion that extends to people, animals, and nature itself. Every encounter, every relationship, and every interaction offer a chance to either uplift or harm. Therefore, if one cannot actively help, it is essential at least to refrain from causing harm. While desire is natural and even necessary for growth, it can serve a higher purpose when directed toward the collective good. Rather than pursuing self-serving desires, one can aspire to bring peace, happiness, and abundance to the world and to protect the environment that sustains life. By seeking the prosperity of their enterprises and the well-being of those within them, they inevitably partake in the larger good, sharing in the growth and abundance that their intentions create.

In the end, humans are here for a reason: to fulfil their potential in the material world while achieving unity with the divine within. This dual purpose, to grow outwardly and deepen inwardly, serves not only the individual but the entire world, bringing harmony, abundance, and peace to all.

Every individual in this world is unique; just as no two leaves are the same, no two people are alike. The primary distinction lies in how plants, animals, and humans operate: plants respond to their environment, animals act instinctively, while only humans possess the ability to "work" and make conscious choices. Unlike plants and animals, which function within nature's laws, humans have free will, allowing them to shape their destinies through the choices they make. They possess empathy, save for the future, harness imagination, and apply logic.

By understanding their strengths and weaknesses, human beings can pursue careers that align with their passions, whether as engineers, doctors, lawyers, environmentalists, chartered accountants, technologists, scientists, monks, businesspeople, and more. Achieving self-actualisation is crucial for realising one's full potential and becoming the best version of oneself—without comparing to others—within their chosen fields. This journey is best undertaken with a spirit of Karma Yoga, contributing positively to the greater good of humanity. The hand that sprinkles rose water on others would automatically spell as roses, isn't it?!

CHAPTER 26
The Power of Beliefs

Beliefs shape who we are, defining our actions and potential. A belief is the acceptance of an idea, whether logical or illogical, and is formed through processes involving reasoning, logical evaluation, memory, emotional influences, and past experiences. Our beliefs are not static; they can be transformed as our attitudes and perspectives change. In essence, a person is a reflection of their beliefs. If you change someone's belief system, you change the person.

Beliefs arise when we hold something as true, guided by our value system, even if the truth of that belief is debatable. For instance, human hearing is limited to a frequency range of 20 Hz to 20,000 Hz, and we perceive light waves within the range of 790 to 400 terahertz. While sound and light extend far beyond these frequencies, our physical senses only allow us to perceive a fraction of these phenomena. Similarly, our beliefs set a threshold for what we can achieve. We accomplish only what we believe we can, reflecting our self-imposed limits.

Humans, however, possess the ability to alter their belief systems based on their aspirations. As the old saying goes, "I think, therefore I am." Extending this concept, if we strongly believe in something, it influences our reality. The universe tends to conspire with us, aligning opportunities and means when we hold unwavering beliefs. The "how" of achieving our desires often emerges seemingly out of nowhere, driven by the strength of our convictions.

To achieve wealth, good health, fulfilment, or even enlightenment, belief in the possibility is essential. However, belief alone is insufficient. Just as dreams can inspire us to build castles in the air, we must remember to lay solid foundations beneath those castles once we awaken. Strong beliefs must be paired with consistent action.

For those with unshakeable beliefs, nothing is impossible. While a rationalist might say, "I'll believe it when I see it," life often teaches us that we must **"first believe"** it to make it visible and real.

With unwavering belief, we can overcome obstacles, conquer fears, tap inner strength, and inspire others.

Here are some inspiring real-life stories showcasing the power of belief:

Overcoming Adversity:

1. Nick Vujicic: Born without limbs, Nick believed in his abilities, becoming a motivational speaker, author, and philanthropist.

2. Stephen Hawking: Diagnosed with ALS, Hawking defied odds, believing in his intellect and publishing groundbreaking research.

3. Bethany Hamilton: Lost her arm surfing, yet believed in her passion, continuing competitive surfing.

Achieving Success:

1. J.K. Rowling: Believed in her writing despite rejections, creating the Harry Potter series.

2. Walt Disney: Fired, bankrupt, yet believed in animation, revolutionising entertainment.

3. Thomas Edison: 1,000 failed experiments didn't deter his belief; he invented the light bulb.

Medical Miracles:

1. Terry Fox: Cancer amputee believed in curing cancer, completing a 3,339-mile marathon.

2. Arunima Sinha: Lost leg, yet believed in becoming the first amputee to climb Mount Everest.

3. Morris Goodman: Paralysed, believed in recovery, learning to walk again.

Inspirational Figures:

1. Malala Yousafzai: Believed in education, survived assassination attempts.

2. Nelson Mandela believed in equality, leading South Africa's transformation.

3. Rosa Parks: Believed in justice, sparking the civil rights movement.

Everyday Heroes:

1. Drew Manning: Believed in empathy, intentionally gaining or losing 75 pounds.

2. Chris Gardner: A homeless single father believed in financial stability and became a stockbroker.

3. Rahmani Ali: Believed in education and taught underprivileged children.

CHAPTER 27
My Spiritual Experiences

1. A Spiritual Connection:

During a brief assignment in late 1984, I found myself entrusted with a task that would test not just my physical limits but also my spiritual resolve. As a site engineer for an electrical contractor, I was responsible for delivering a sealed tender to the administrative office of the Sriharikota Space Centre—a feat made daunting by the wrath of an intense cyclone with torrential rains and 150 km/h winds.

The journey began with obstacles: uprooted trees, blocked roads, and a disrupted train service that delayed my arrival. Despite the chaos of the storm, a deep sense of purpose anchored me, propelling me forward with unwavering determination. Each step of my journey, from a reluctant lorry driver offering me a ride to running the last eight kilometres against the fury of the elements, felt guided by an unseen force. It was as if the storm, nature's mightiest challenge, was testing not just my endurance but my faith. I was all alone on the road running about 8 km. I ran as if I was possessed by a strange force weathering all the vagaries of the North East monsoon!!

Arriving at the office with mere minutes to spare, soaked and exhausted, I handed over the tender, only to learn that the deadline had been extended by a week. The irony was palpable, but in that moment of realisation, I felt an overwhelming connection to something far greater than myself. It was not about the tender or the contract; it was about the journey—one that demanded absolute commitment, perseverance, and surrender to a higher power.

Reflecting on this experience, I felt the presence of the divine in every challenge I overcame. The storm mirrored the turbulence of life, and yet, through the sheer intensity of purpose, I had navigated it. The labour of my commitment became a prayer, and the sweat of my effort transformed into a symbol of grace. It wasn't merely about succeeding in the task but about rising in my own eyes—knowing that I had been part of a larger design, connected to the spiritual realm in ways words could scarcely capture.

As Mahatria beautifully says, "If you are committed to a principle so much so that you wouldn't mind risking your life for it, the sheer intensity of your commitment would make life adapt to you rather than you adapting to life." That day, I realised that my spine of commitment was not just holding me upright but was aligning me with the divine, reaffirming that even amidst life's storms, a higher power guides those who dare to persevere.

2. A Sacred Ascent – A Journey Beyond Myself

In August 2024, I embarked on a deeply spiritual journey to Sabarimala, a revered temple nestled in the Western Ghats of Kerala. As I reached Pamba, the base of the hill leading to the sanctum sanctorum of Lord Ayyappa, I felt a profound sense of anticipation and reverence. The climb of about 4.5 kilometres awaited me—a path I had traversed before in about an hour and fifteen minutes. But this time, the heavens opened in an unrelenting downpour.

What began as a gentle drizzle soon transformed into a massive deluge, obscuring visibility to less than 10 feet. Armed only with a shoulder bag and an umbrella, I felt both vulnerable and resolute. Each step I took felt like a prayer, an offering of faith to something far greater than myself. The rain was not just a challenge—it became a cleansing force, stripping away distractions and grounding me in the present moment.

With each step, I focused on the 5 feet of path ahead, unable to see further but fully trusting the journey. My faith in Lord Ayyappa and the divine energy of the temple filled me with strength, guiding me upwards despite the challenges. The rhythm of my steps mirrored the rhythm of my prayers, and in those moments, I felt deeply connected to the spiritual realm.

It was as though the rain, the climb, and the sacred destination were all elements of a larger, divine design. The downpour, far from deterring me, felt like a symbol of surrender—a reminder that life's storms can also be pathways to profound connection. By the time I reached the sanctum, drenched yet fulfilled, I realised that the journey was not just about physical endurance but about experiencing the divine within and around me.

Each step was an act of devotion, and the climb became a metaphor for life's spiritual ascent—anchored in faith, guided by unseen forces, and illuminated by the divine presence I sought to experience in Lord Ayyappa's sacred abode.

CHAPTER 28
Some Spiritual Practices That Could Be Incorporated into Daily Life

Morning Practices

1. Meditation (5-15 minutes).

2. Yoga or stretching.

3. Pranayama.

4. Prayer or intention setting

5. Gratitude journaling.

6. Connecting with nature (e.g., walking, gardening).

Throughout the Day

1. Mindfulness: Focus on the present moment

2. Acts of kindness and compassion.

Evening Practices

1. Reflection on the day's events.

2. Forgiveness and letting go.

3. Reading spiritual texts or scriptures.

4. Journaling or writing.

5. Candlelight or fire meditation.

Daily Habits

1. Practice non-judgement and acceptance.

2. Cultivate self-awareness and self-compassion.

3. Engage in selfless service (e.g. volunteering).

4. Connect with others through empathy and listening.

5. Prioritise self-care and well-being

Spiritual Disciplines

1. Fasting once in a while.

2. Simple living and minimalism.

3. Digital detox or limited screen time.

4. Solitude and quiet time.

This book, "The Essence of Spirituality" by Brother Ramkumar, former General Manager at the Headquarters of the International Theosophical Society Adyar, covers the field of unfoldment of consciousness (the Divine plan) with a practical approach to spiritual path in a simple way.

In this book, Ramkumar writes about meditation, stages of meditation, benefits of meditation, types of meditation and techniques of meditation, which i think are most useful for the readers to know how to quieten the mind from its restlessness and to lead a peaceful life in this changing life stream.

The book becomes more interesting as it includes examples of real-life inspiring stories of Nelson Mandela, Mahatma Gandhi, sports icons, business leaders and their essential steps in spirituality.

Prof C.A. Shinde, International speaker,
Theosophical Society